The Gift of Life:
The Story of Edward Pompeian and the Founding of the Gift of Life Transplant House
By Edward P. Pompeian
With Ricky Sprague

Sister Briana, for
Thank you years volunteer
all of your and Life
of ministry of
work at Gift House.
Transplant and
Best wishes
God Bless.

Edward P. Pompeian
6-27-17
Jayne Pompeian

This book is dedicated to my loving wife Jayne, who has been an integral part of my transplant journey and the writing of my story.

ISBN-13: 978-1537304151

ISBN-10: 1537304151

For more information on the Gift of Life Transplant House and the Mayo Clinic, please visit the following websites:

http://gift-of-life.org/

http://www.mayoclinic.org/

Contents

"Start by doing what is necessary, then do what is possible, and suddenly you are doing the impossible."
-St. Francis of Assisi

Prologue

On two picturesque campuses in Rochester, Minnesota, less than half a mile from the world-renowned Mayo Clinic, organ, bone marrow, and stem cell transplant patients and their families can find comfort and support in what can be an arduous and highly stressful time. For over thirty years countless volunteers, wonderful staff with great hearts, and generous donors have contributed to its success. Thanks to their tireless efforts guests get the care and respect they need in a "home away from home." Each room has two beds and includes amenities such as private bathrooms, heating and cooling, writing desks, closet space, and more. In addition, the facilities boast communal areas that allow the patients to interact with each other, sharing stories of hope and encouragement.

Transplant recipients stay for anywhere from a few weeks to four months or even longer, depending on need. The Gift of Life Transplant House asks for $30 per day from those who can afford it. If patients arrive when the house is full, staff will help them find discounted accommodations at nearby hotels until a guest room opens up.

The eighty-seven bedrooms in more than eighty-eight thousand square feet of buildings bear little resemblance to the comparatively modest eight-bedroom house at West Center Street that first bore the name Gift of Life Transplant House. When I first conceived of it, I had no way of knowing it would grow to become the largest transplant house program in the country. Guided by God's hand and motivated by my own personal health struggles, I dreamed that I could help others overcome the obstacles that I faced before I received my own gift of life.

The 705 House

The 724 House

Chapter One: "Your son will not live to be sixteen."

Walking through the front door, I knew.

This was the place. A beautiful eight-bedroom, three story Craftsman style house with all the original woodwork. It needed a lot of work, but it was a strong, solid structure that conveyed a sense of durability and warmth. More than that, this was a home. *God had guided me to this place as part of His plan—even if I hadn't understood.*

But after that initial rush of excitement, I was struck by practical considerations. My wife Jayne and I had just had our first son a year before, and our second child was due in December. I was only six years into building my own real estate business. Money wasn't plentiful at this time, and there was so much that required my time and attention. But these obstacles were nothing compared with what I knew to be my mission.

This was the perfect environment for a transplant house.

The transplant journey is long and difficult, and patients and their families face a number of daunting challenges, even beyond the actual medical procedures involved. I had experienced these hardships firsthand. My desire to help others on their transplant journey arose from my own experiences, and my values were instilled in me from an early age thanks to the compassionate, giving example of my mother, Helen.

Pontiac, Michigan in the 1950s and '60s was a wonderful area in which to grow up. It was the heyday of the American automotive industry, and Pontiac was one of the chief beneficiaries of a booming economy. This small town was filled with welcoming neighborhoods where you knew your neighbors for an entire city block. Kids played sidewalk games, baseball, hide and seek, and kickball. It seemed like anything was possible, and I was a happy, healthy boy who enthusiastically took advantage of every opportunity for fun and friendship.

At the time central Michigan had a large Armenian population, and this tight-knit group placed a strong emphasis on our shared traditions, faith in God, and the foundational importance of family. I attended an Armenian school until I was about six years old. My sister Sharon and I were members of Pontiac's Armenian Youth Federation chapter. My mother Helen was a member of the Armenian Relief Society. She had four sisters (Janet, May, Alice, and Isabel) and two brothers (Richard and Paul), and family friends were the people she grew up with, who would remain friends their entire lives. They often got together for special occasions such as holidays, birthdays, and picnics. Armenian food was at the center of these gatherings; my father, Edward Sr., enjoyed making an Armenian shish kebab called a taskabab. Christmas and Thanksgiving meals always centered around classic turkey, but with plenty of Armenian dishes including rice and bulgur pilaf.

My Armenian friends and family created a loving support structure. Our heritage provided us with a reservoir of strength from which to draw—this strength would prove to be a vital component of my survival.

Sharon, five years my senior, was ecstatic when our mother brought me home from the hospital. The two of us shared a bedroom in our two-bedroom duplex—and our maternal grandmother lived upstairs. The deep, abiding love between Sharon and me was untouched by any sibling jealousy. Our only source of conflict arose when Sharon would hide her candy in her dresser. "It's bad for you, anyway!" she'd tell me, laughing.

I got good grades in school, and I got along really well with my classmates. Until I was eleven years old, I insisted that everyone in my class be invited to my birthday parties, to ensure no one felt left out.

Between me and my mother there was a connection that went beyond the typical mother-son bond. I loved to sing while she played the piano, and she'd often wait for me on the porch when I came home from school, cheerfully whistling a happy tune.

There was no reason for any of us to think this idyllic world could be shattered, and the family would face terrible hardship that would threaten my life for years to come.

The beginning of what my mother would call our family's nightmare occurred during a typical family outing—a visit to one of the first shopping centers in the United States, Northland Center in the Detroit suburb Southfield. This regular monthly trip included our mother, maternal grandmother, and aunt Janet. Our mother took me and Sharon to Hudson's—now Macy's—where we would have lunch, shop, and I would be allowed to pick out one new toy, book, or game.

We stood in line at the cafeteria-style restaurant inside the department store, talking and laughing. I started to respond to a teasing remark that Sharon had made when I was suddenly overcome by a feeling of intense nausea. Before I could process what was happening to my body, I began to vomit.

The family did their best to comfort me. But it wasn't long before the nausea was accompanied by feelings of lethargy, and I was overwhelmed by debilitating pain. On the drive back home I started running a high fever. When we returned home my mother called our family doctor, who advised her to bring me to his office immediately.

The doctor performed an examination, but he was unable to make a diagnosis. He prescribed sulfa, which he believed would lower my temperature and help to ease my pain. Unfortunately, this was the beginning of what was to become a frustrating and dangerous pattern in my life: Missed diagnoses and ineffective treatments.

Over the next few weeks, my condition showed only incremental improvement. Then, I suddenly began getting sicker. Still confused as to what was happening, our doctor advised us to go to the emergency room at the Cottage Hospital in Grosse Pointe, Michigan. After a battery of tests, the doctors diagnosed strep throat, pneumonia, and a treatable form of kidney disease called lupus nephritis. I received high doses of steroids and Chloroquine, a drug typically used to treat malaria but whose side effects can include aches and pains, and blurred vision.

As hopeful as my family was about the diagnosis and treatment, what was perhaps the best thing about this trip to the hospital was that it served as the means by which Sam and Mary Ann Leto entered our lives.

The Letos were a devoutly Catholic couple who would grow to become very close to me and my family. Mary was at the hospital recuperating from a serious illness, and she and Sam spent a great deal of time with me. Among the conversation topics was Padre Pio of Pietrelcina, a priest in Italy renowned for his healing powers, who would become a Saint in 2002. Sam had several medals he'd received from this pious man, and he felt these medals had aided him in his own recovery. He presented them to me, and suggested that I write Padre Pio a letter asking him to pray for me. Padre Pio responded to my letter, telling me that he would remember me in his prayers, and enclosed with his reply a small picture that I would carry with me for many years, a tangible reminder of the Padre's help.

Another topic of conversation was the Mayo Clinic.

Sam explained that the doctors and researchers were doing

remarkable work for those dealing with serious illness—including Sam himself, who'd suffered from kidney problems years before. The Letos described the clinic and its specialists, covering nearly every field of medicine and research.

However, in this period of high stress, Sam's advice made little impact. This was to be a continuing source of regret for my mother who, fatigued and distraught, was being crushed under the weight of the information she was hearing from the various doctors and nurses we encountered—all while dealing with the startling changes that were affecting my body. It was difficult for her to fully process this whirlwind of painful and confusing events. The Mayo Clinic information seemed no more remarkable than everything else we were hearing at this time.

Then, a fearful accumulation of bodily fluid caused my abdomen to become distended. With her conversations with Sam in the back of her mind, my mother asked the attending physician if I should be moved to another facility where they'd be able to provide better care. The doctor replied, "I know of no other place. If I did, I would tell you."

This dismissal had a profound impact on my mother, who trusted that my doctors were doing the best they could and providing the best available care and information.

After returning home, I was briefly able to return to junior high school. Unfortunately, my mysterious illness only worsened, and no one could understand why. As the questions about my condition intensified, so did my family's fear.

Days stretched into weeks and then, gradually, into years. Uncertainty and anxiety seemed to dog us at every step. There were brief respites of peace, but the dangerous reality of my condition was inescapable.

Finally, when I was fourteen, doctors advised that I be taken to a hospital with a children's ward. The plan was for yet another round in the seemingly endless array of tests to which I'd already been subjected. When my mother and father took me, by wheelchair, to the huge room full of sick, lonely children, I recoiled in horror. My mother knew that if they left me in this place I would lose all hope. Taking her hand, I looked at her and gasped, "Mom, do I have to stay here?"

Seeing me like that broke her heart. It was several seconds before she was able to finally find her voice. They couldn't leave me here. They wouldn't leave me here. Despite the danger, they knew that I stood a far better chance of recovery at home than in this desolate children's ward that seemed so devoid of compassion.

I tried to remain upbeat. But the rest of my family was beginning to lose hope. Occasionally I would smile and ask, "Am I doing all right?"

Their answers were reassuring, but the fact was, I was *not* doing all right. My condition seemed to worsen with each passing day. My physical pain was nearly matched by the relentless emotional anguish that my mother, father, and sister experienced seeing my suffering and not being able to do anything to stop it.

A family friend suggested that I be taken to another doctor. After a brief examination I was taken to yet another hospital, and forced to endure even more tests. This went on for five grueling weeks, with my mother remaining by my side nearly every minute of the day and night. On top of everything else, there was a horrible new development: back pain so great it nearly overshadowed all of my other ailments. An X-ray revealed a compression fracture in my lower spine.

More tests. More prescriptions. More treatments. Nothing helped. In fact, my condition deteriorated. Slowly my vision blurred and dimmed, to the point that I was nearly blind. I was so weak I couldn't move from my bed under my own power. And my face and body were now covered in a painful rash.

My mother was devastated when she heard me whisper, in a voice barely audible: "Mom, I came here with a backache, and I can tell my insides are very sick. Please get me out of here."

The words cut her, but they were nothing compared to what one of the doctors told her. He called her into the lobby and in a matter-of-fact, purely clinical tone, he said:

"Your son will not live to be sixteen. You should be glad you've had him this long."

She felt the world spinning, as all the oxygen seemed to leave the room. Her body became weak. A great sadness gripped her, and she began to tremble.

Soon she realized she wasn't trembling out of fear or sadness—but anger. Anger for the doctor standing before her, who seemed wholly devoid of anything even remotely related to compassion. Anger over a situation that seemed to grow more confusing by the day. Anger over the fact that after yet another five weeks of tests she and her family had no hope, no answers—only a dispassionate statement that her son would soon be dead and this doctor, this *man* standing before her was unable and perhaps even uninterested in doing anything to help.

With no diagnosis and a child who now seemed sicker than ever, the family returned home, hoping that the God who had given me the strength to endure this illness would also provide us with the guidance to find the answers we needed to help me get well.

Your son will not live to be sixteen.

The callous statement echoed in my mother's mind. It would haunt her for years. To her, it came to symbolize the hubris of the doctors who never suggested that there might be alternatives to the care they were providing. Their attitude seemed to be, *If we can't help him, well, he is simply beyond help.* Even in her darkest moments, she never succumbed to their attitude of hopelessness.

Your son will not live to be sixteen.

Some of the members of our family seemed resigned to the idea that I would never regain my health. Surely, if there were another medical center that could provide us with superior care, one of the myriad of doctors and nurses we'd encountered through the years would have told us of this.

Despite what the Letos had said about the Mayo Clinic, to my mother it seemed little more than an abstraction. Not a real place, but somewhere far off in the distance—lost in the haze of pain and fear that enveloped our lives.

Your son will not live to be sixteen.

All along I understood the profound threat I was facing. What I'd lived through, no child should have to endure. From yet another hospital bed, I looked up at my mother and said, "Mom, something terrible is happening to me. I feel worse and worse, and if you don't get me out of here, you will see my death notice in the paper. Please take me to the Mayo Clinic. Don't listen to anyone. Just get me out of here. Remember what Mary and Sam said: that I'd have a better chance there to get well.

"Please, Mom, don't wait. I can't eat; I can hardly see; I hurt everywhere. Please, please, Mom—hurry and call the Mayo Clinic before it is too late."

At that moment, my mother realized that she'd put far too much stock in what the doctors had told her.

Your son will—

The echoing stopped; my words now overwhelmed every other consideration. My mother felt her heart pounding; her only thought was to return home and call the Mayo Clinic. She went immediately to the parking lot. In her rush to leave, she inadvertently drove over a cement divider, immobilizing the car. Without thinking she got out of the car and ran home, only to discover that she'd left the keys in the ignition. She ran back to retrieve the keys, then ran home again, with a feeling of frantic exhaustion.

Finally, back home, she made the call. Nearly terrified at the prospect of putting me in further danger, she wondered if the Mayo Clinic would truly be able to help. And even if they could, would I actually survive the journey?

After explaining my situation, they agreed to see me as soon as I could be moved to Worrall Hospital, which was then a part of the Mayo facility, in downtown Rochester.

The administrative staff at my current hospital made it clear that they didn't want me to leave. One of them told us that if I were discharged, my family would assume full responsibility for my care.

I was thrilled to be on my way, and the entire family took heart from my newfound optimism. Not even an airline strike dampened our spirits, as my father secured the services of a private plane that would fly us to Rochester.

But the reality of our situation, and the danger I was facing, hit us with full force once we'd returned home from the hospital. My vision was still failing. I was still suffering with great pain. My entire body was covered with a red, itchy rash. My speech was slurred. I was unable to retain food. I couldn't walk. I was suffering with obesity, weakness in my arms and legs, and osteoporosis.

Sitting beside my bed in our living room, my mother fought hard to suppress her tears. I reached out to touch her face, and tried to reassure her that the trip to the Mayo Clinic was the right choice.

Feeling exhausted and terrified, she rose from her chair and stepped across the room, to spare me having to deal with her agony.

Sharon said, "Mom, don't worry; I'll take care of you and Edward." When my mother's courage faltered, she provided encouragement and support.

Everyone in the family was on edge. My grandmother had been a constant source of encouragement throughout the ordeal;

now, even she was silent. She feared that this was the last she would see her grandson alive.

Me, my sister Sharon, my father Edward Sr,
and my mother Helen

Sam and Mary Ann Leto

Me and Sharon as kids

Me and Sharon today

Chapter Two: There is much to be thankful for

It was perfect. But how could I possibly pay for it?

Surveying the house, I tried to come up with an answer. Then, in a flash of inspiration that must have been divinely inspired, I turned to the owner, Mrs. Cunningham, and explained my dream of using this property for a transplant house. I told her of my own struggles. I told her of the people that I'd met throughout the course of my various treatments, and the camaraderie and affection that developed between us. I explained that those who required transplant surgeries faced expensive obstacles, struggling to find affordable housing near the Clinic while also making rent or mortgage payments on their own properties back home—all while having to take time off from work. Giving these people an affordable place to stay would make a major impact on their lives, meaning they'd have one less thing to worry about on their transplant journey.

She loved the idea of her home being used for this purpose, but she needed some of the proceeds in order to finance the purchase of her new home.

I told her that I didn't yet have the money to buy her house. I asked her for the minimum amount she needed in order to buy her new home.

"Fifteen thousand dollars," was her reply.

I wrote out an agreement to buy the home for $100,000, with a $15,000 down payment. She agreed to finance the balance on a five-year installment sale, with a balloon payment at the end of the five years.

At this point I had no idea where I'd get that full amount, but my life story was one of overcoming seemingly insurmountable obstacles. I'd faced down greater difficulties than this and, with God's help, I'd always managed to succeed. This would be no different. I knew God had been watching over me my entire life.

The night before we left for Rochester, my mother had a dream that would hold great significance for her, and provide her with the strength she needed to make that first trip to the Mayo Clinic. In the dream God appeared before her, holding out His hands to her. "Take this," He said. All she could see was His long flowing robe, and the hands reaching out. As her hands touched His, a glowing light appeared, then slowly faded away.

The light inspired her.

She was awakened by a sound that seemed to come from somewhere far away. It took her several moments to realize it was the sound of the doorbell. Waiting on the porch was my father, and standing beside him was a police officer who explained that he had been involved in an automobile accident. Although my father hadn't been injured, the car was totaled.

The trip to Rochester was now only a few hours away, so when the family had finished talking through the accident, we remained awake to discuss the preparations for the trip.

I required a great deal of assistance during this difficult time. I was on an incredible number of medicines, each of which needed to be administered on its own tightly controlled schedule. Trip logistics—including actually moving me—carried their own particular burdens. My excruciating pain, in particular the pain in my back, meant that special care needed to be taken at all times. Neighbors and family members offered vital assistance. Sharon was especially helpful, taking it upon herself to ensure everything was done to ready me for the trip.

My delicate condition meant it was essential that I be kept flat on my back, on a stretcher. I was taken by ambulance to the chartered plane at the airport where attendants helped me board and then get to the bed where I had to lie on my side. My mother sat beside my body, administering medicine as necessary. Sharon was always close by, and not just for moral support.

Space was cramped within the small propeller plane. The engine was loud—too loud for conversation—and the plane flew low, making for a bumpy and long trip. We were in the air for more than four hours. Overall, the flight was a harrowing experience.

At the Rochester airport we were met by another ambulance that took us to Worrall Hospital. The doctors there were shocked by my condition. Tests revealed that the previous diagnosis of lupus nephritis had been dangerously wrong. Not only were the steroids and other medications I'd been prescribed *not* helping me, they were causing major complications.

Following this initial battery of tests, I was taken to Saint Marys Hospital. At long last, I was getting care from doctors who had a handle on my condition, and a diagnosis was finally made: Glomerulonephritis. This is an inflammation of the glomeruli—the filters inside the kidneys that facilitate removal of waste from the bloodstream—and is a deadly condition that can take many forms. In my case, it had caused advanced renal failure. One of my kidneys had completely ceased functioning; the other kidney was only functioning at one-quarter strength.

By this time my kidneys were damaged beyond repair. The doctors told me it was only a matter of time before my kidneys failed completely, and that I would need dialysis and a transplant in the future.

As heartbreaking as this news was, my mother was grateful for the doctors at Worrall and Saint Marys Hospitals. She felt a wave of relief that at least now we finally had some understanding of what was happening to my body. Yet, she couldn't help but feel anger at the doctors in Michigan, who'd forced me to endure a seemingly endless battery of surgeries, tests, and medicines. And all the while, my condition had only worsened. None of those doctors made any effort to reach out to specialists who might have been able to shed some light on the "mystery" of my condition. Yet again, she was haunted by the doctor's words:

Your son will not live to be sixteen.

All along, the treatments this and the other doctors had prescribed had actually been weakening me. She came to believe that it was a miracle I'd endured long enough to get the care and treatment I needed at the Mayo Clinic.

Although by this time I was very sick, the doctors told my mother that they believed I had every chance for a full recovery. It would be a long and difficult process, but already I was showing tentative signs of alertness. Slowly my mother began to notice that feelings of hope were pushing aside her fears. She was able to draw strength from these promising signs of my progress, the memory of her vision of God, and from the devoted family and friends who offered so much love and support.

*

My father had found my mother a room across the street from the hospital. Every morning she came to visit me, and often remained by my side until well into the night. The nurses would place me on a cart so I would lie flat on my back. This was actually a tricky, time-consuming process, owing to the fact that my back was in an almost constant state of agony.

My mother would wheel me up and down the halls in an attempt to stimulate me, and get me interested in my new surroundings. Usually, I gave little indication that I was aware of what was happening. Even as I was showing signs of improvement, I rarely spoke; I was just too weak. But I was grateful beyond words for these moments with her.

Then one day, while we were traveling the hallway, I was able to find my voice. I looked up at her and said, "Mom, I'm feeling a lot better, and everyone is so nice to me. Why don't you go home?"

The words were like a panacea to her. She understood that I was no longer afraid for my life, and wanted her to get the rest she so desperately needed. She was able to sleep a little easier that night, knowing that I was coming out of danger.

Nevertheless, the years of stress that she had endured had a cumulative effect. She couldn't shake her worry, and she felt ragged and tired almost all the time. Sharon's encouragement was vital, but there came a time when she had to return to Pontiac to go back to school.

After one particularly trying day, I kept urging my mother to return to her own room to get some rest. Finally, around ten o'clock, she left my room. But she couldn't quite bring herself to leave the hospital.

Emotionally and physically drained, she sat in the hospital lobby. She tried to read, but the words on the page meant nothing to her. She felt completely detached from the world. She'd spent so much time in hospitals and by my bedside, puzzling over my condition and doing everything she could to help me. It seemed like her entire life revolved around me and my illness.

She needed a sympathetic ear. She called one of her sisters in Michigan who offered support and asked all the right questions about my condition, but her words did nothing to alleviate the accumulated hurt. There was no way that her sister could truly understand the stress that had come to define her life, even with my hopeful signs of recovery.

Without saying goodbye, my mother put down the receiver. A fearful sense of dejection overwhelmed her as she made her way back to the lobby. Feeling confused and frightened, she returned to her seat. At that moment she felt a gentle hand on her shoulder, and a voice said, "Mrs. Pompeian, are you all right?"

She broke down. When she was finally able to speak again, the words flowed from her in a torrent, and the caring woman—who turned out to be one of my nurses—listened attentively, offering sympathy and support until my mother was able to regain control.

She understood how much her worry had worn her down, but she also explained to my mother that it was crucial that she get the rest she needed. She told her that she would be acting as my nurse the following morning, and to focus not on the stressful and confusing past, but on the reassuring future.

The nurse's words resonated with my mother, and she was finally able to return to her room. The next morning, she got the hopeful news that her Sister May would soon be coming to visit, and that their mother would also be coming to Rochester to spend time with her.

*

My mother's decision to focus on the positives for the future was bolstered by my own brightening attitude. As she stepped into my room that morning, she saw a cheerful light shining in my eyes. I'd spent all morning coming up with a plan that I felt would go a long way toward helping me heal emotionally if not physically.

"Mom, I know I can sit in a wheelchair!" I told her, excitedly. "I'm going to ask the nurse if I can. I know she'll think it's a good idea. And then will you take me down the hall so I can play pool? I want to play pool with some of my new friends!"

I know that my mother had almost given up hope that she'd ever again hear me speak with such enthusiasm and hope in my voice. Happily, the nurses agreed that the wheelchair was a good idea, at least on a trial basis. It turned out to be an amazing morale boost for me, and I had a lot of fun helping my mother navigate the halls, and greeting everyone we met on our travels.

On our regular trips up and down the Saint Marys Hospital hallways my mother and I slowly became acquainted with the other children and their mothers. One of the children with whom I shared a special connection was a five year-old Korean girl, a tiny, fragile child suffering from leukemia. I loved to make her laugh at my jokes, and she appreciated the companionship. She often begged her parents to take her to my room.

As the girl's condition worsened and she became more and more fragile, I decided I had to do something special for her. In a solemn tone, I told my mother that I needed a favor. I wanted to get the girl a present—something that I hoped she would really like. The two of us talked it over and decided that a doll would be the perfect gift. My mother went to the store and found a pretty, cuddly doll that she thought the girl would enjoy.

When we entered the girl's room, I sang out playfully, "I brought you something! Can you guess what it is?"

She smiled. "Something nice! Can I have it, Eddie?"

Her small hands reached out and took the doll, hugging it to her. Over and over she said, "Look what Eddie brought me! Look what Eddie brought me!"

The girl's parents, my mother, and I watched her, sensing her genuine pleasure. We were happy to be able to help her, even if only in a small way. But it was clear that the girl's strength was waning. It served as a reminder of the fact that, despite everything we'd been through, my mother and I both had a great deal to be thankful for.

Chapter Three: Milestones

For selling the house I received a three thousand-dollar commission, meaning I had 20% of the funds needed for the down payment. I went to my best friend Norm Gillette, a transplant recipient who was also the owner of a Pepsi franchise. Norm offered to match my three thousand, which meant that now I was up to forty percent.

From there, I went to all of the contacts I'd made through my real estate business, as well as those I'd met through the Mayo Clinic.

Slowly but surely, I raised the funds I needed, and I was able to make the down payment. With God's help, I had the house. However, I'd been so focused on the acquisition of the facility that I'd given little thought to how it would be operated. I had no more money, no board, and no name for the house!

Although I was reaching one milestone after another, I seemed to encounter further obstacles. It was a familiar pattern throughout my life.

During my time at Saint Marys, every aspect of my ongoing treatment was meticulously planned. This careful strategy had the desired effect and gradually, my strength began to return. Although no one could predict when I might be walking again under my own power, a therapy was designed to strengthen my muscles. I began walking between parallel bars while using my hands for support; this became an important part of my daily routine.

The compression fracture made it necessary for me to wear a specially designed back brace for six months. Removing and replacing this brace was a difficult procedure not only because of my back pain, but also because of my extremely sensitive skin.

Also vital to my recuperation were my regular wheelchair trips through the hospital corridors. As awkward as it was from my wheelchair, I especially loved being able to play pool in the playroom.

Some of the most difficult accommodations revolved around my diet. Gone was my seemingly endless array of prescribed medicines. But they'd been replaced by a highly specialized and stringent eating regimen that limited me to a single ounce of protein a day, and no salt. My mother had to make a low protein bread that seemed to share both the properties and taste of rubber. This could be eaten with a little salt-free peanut butter and jelly, and nothing else.

As hard as it was for me to eat, my diet's preparation and planning was a time-consuming process. My mother had to shop so as to be certain she always had the necessary ingredients on hand, and ensure she had plenty of cooking time.

My improvement was noticeable to everyone and, after eight weeks, the doctors felt comfortable letting me return home to Pontiac. What a difference those two months had made!

Mayo's doctors told my mother to remain in touch and provide them with regular updates about my health. They explained that when transplant technology had progressed far enough they would let us know when to come for a transplant.

My mother was relieved that God had heard her prayers, and she sent Him a heartfelt thanks for everything He'd done for me.

Upon our return, we were warmly and joyously received by our family and friends. Unfortunately, we barely had time to catch our breath and appreciate our blessings before a terrible tragedy overwhelmed me with grief.

My friend Eddie McKerricher and I had been playmates and school friends for most of our lives. From an early age, we'd known we wanted to travel together, and seeing Eddie again was a major motivation in my quest to get better.

Then came the awful news: Eddie McKerricher had drowned.

I was heartbroken, and plunged into a fearful sorrow that threatened my recovery. Despite my mother's objections, I insisted on going to the funeral. She worried about the emotional and physical damage that the trip might inflict on me. Her concern was appreciated and completely understandable; however, she and the rest of my family soon came to realize that denying me the chance to say goodbye to my friend could be just as hurtful—perhaps more so. Sharon took me to the jewelry store, where I purchased a small gold cross for Eddie to wear.

The funeral was a celebration of Eddie's life, mixed with mournful thoughts of what might have been. Devastated family and friends gathered to pay their respects, commiserate, and say goodbye. In keeping with Armenian tradition, dinner was served.

It was during this sad occasion that Sharon met the young man who would eventually become her husband, and the father of her son Paul.

*

For a long time, I had trouble dealing with the shock and grief I felt over the loss of my dear friend. My mother had hoped that

21

soon I would recover enough to want to play with my many toys and games. But I surprised her when I told her that I no longer wished to keep them. Holding on to a few items of particular sentimental value, I gave some things to my friends, then had a sale to dispense with the rest.

Looking back I realize that getting rid of my toys was a symbolic but important gesture. It was a sign that I was moving on with my life, entering a new phase of my recovery. Soon it was time for me to step into a new school arrangement. Some of my previous teachers graciously agreed to evaluate my interest and skill level, and crafted assignments that a tutor helped me complete. My mother then took the completed work to the teachers to be graded.

I was slowly getting back into an education routine, but before I could actually attend class, it was crucial that I build up my physical strength. To that end, an attendant would come to our home, lift me from my bed, and carry me to the van. My mother and I were then driven to the hospital, where I worked diligently on an exercise program that was focused on building my strength and stamina so I could move under my own power once again.

This was a precarious time. As she watched me, my mother couldn't help but to cast her mind back to the time before all the pain—a time when I would run and jump and play with my friends. I'd loved school so much! Now just taking a few steps was an agonizing struggle, but I was determined to return to school.

As my mobility improved, my father promised me that as soon as I was able to walk from the bedroom to the living room under my own power, he'd get me a new color television set. This turned out to be a strong motivator, and the new TV was a happy addition to my life.

But I was still looking forward to the day when I could resume my school life. One day near Christmas, I got a wonderful reminder that my schoolmates and teachers were equally anxious to see me return. The school's highly regarded music teacher brought my class to our family home to sing carols. I was surprised and delighted by the gesture, and as my family and the students shared spiced apple juice and cookies, I felt a renewed determination to get back to school.

Finally, at long last, I was strong enough to once again attend classes. It wasn't long before I settled into a routine at Washington Junior High School, working toward making up the work I'd missed. I belonged in school, and I took advantage of every opportunity my health would allow, reconnecting with old friends and making new ones.

Unfortunately, when graduation day arrived, I was still too weak to walk in the graduate procession. The school's principal delivered my diploma to me at home. This gracious gesture meant a lot to the entire family.

From there, I was ready for high school. I understood that this was a major milestone in my life—one which many thought I'd never live to see. Just growing up, living one day at time, meant a great deal to me, and I felt gratitude and appreciation for every minute of it. At the same time, my health made it impossible for me to do many of the things my fellow students could do. Even going up and down steps was an exhausting hazard, meaning that very soon after the start of my freshman year I had to leave Pontiac Central High School in favor of Pontiac Northern High School.

In 1968, my family moved from Pontiac to Birmingham, Michigan. Because I wanted to finish high school with the same friends and teachers, I drove myself back and forth from Birmingham to Pontiac Northern.

Through it all—the desperate sickness, the recovery, and the change in school—I never lost my love of learning. I'd always clung to the hope that one day I'd be well enough to return to school, make friends, and live as normal a life as possible, despite my delicate health.

In the end I didn't just complete high school—I was blessed to be able to graduate with honors. On May 13, 1969, we received a letter from the principal, Philip J. Wargelin. It read in part:

It's our pleasure to advise you that Edward has been elected to membership in the National Honor Society at Pontiac Northern High School. This selection was made by a faculty committee on the basis of demonstrated qualities of character, service, scholarship, and leadership. Kindly accept our congratulations on this significant achievement, for this is a credit to you and the home which is represented…

By continuing to focus on the future I was passing one milestone after another, and thriving, despite all the obstacles in my path. Now I was ready to tackle another challenge and embark on my college career. Unfortunately, my most deadly tests still lay ahead.

Chapter Four: Pain and hope

Trusting that God would be with me, I forged ahead.

I met with another transplant recipient, an attorney named Mark Torgrimson. I persuaded Mark to help me form the business entity that would oversee administration of the house. Mark and his firm agreed to perform all the legal work for free.

After a lengthy discussion we settled on Gift of Life, Inc. for the name of the entity. The home would be called the Gift of Life Transplant House.

Mary Davie, who worked at Mayo, had been a trusted confidante and provided encouragement and advice throughout the process. Now I talked with her about potential board members. Mayo's chief transplant surgeon and head of the program, Dr. Sylvester Sterioff, had given us assistance almost from the beginning of our quest to build a transplant house, so we asked him to serve on the board as vice president. Greg Warner, head of the dialysis center, was asked to serve as president. Mary would serve as secretary and I would act as treasurer.

The Gift of Life House was now much more than just a dream. Slowly, it was becoming a reality.

Having graduated high school with honors, it was time to spread my wings and move into the world of higher education. Like most adolescents I was anxious to leave home, and I managed to convince my family that I was ready to take this important step. I had to promise to always consider my physical limitations, and always be near a phone in case of emergencies.

In the fall of 1969, I started attending classes at Adrian College, a small liberal arts college located about eighty miles southwest of Birmingham in Adrian, Michigan. I loved this new life in the dorm, where I made new friends and enjoyed as many activities as possible.

Then, in one horrifying instant, everything changed.

I was sitting in class just like any other day. All at once the world around me seemed to lose all solidity and then suddenly—

—I was lying on the floor beside my desk, covered in sweat, my body shaking.

My classmates and teacher told me that I had begun to convulse madly, and then I passed out. Just as when my illness first manifested on that fateful day at Hudson's, I simply lost control of my body. I was taken directly to a hospital, where my mother was called.

As soon as she hung up the phone, my mother ran out to the car. She double-checked her purse, to ensure she had money in case she needed it. Since she only had a few dollars, she quickly ran back to the house and grabbed her checkbook, then went back to the car.

Still frantic, her mind raced with thoughts of worry—and all the while, her foot pressed harder on the accelerator. After several hours of driving, she began to wonder why it was taking her so long to reach Adrian. She pulled over at a gas station in Jackson, Michigan and learned she'd driven well out of her way and would need to backtrack. Her worry only increased.

Noticing she was running low on gas, she told the attendant to fill up the tank, hurriedly made out the check, then got detailed directions back to Adrian. As she drove away, she was vaguely aware that the attendant wore an amused expression, but to the extent she processed it at all, she attributed it to his reaction to her confused exasperation. Her focus was on reaching me.

When she finally arrived at the hospital, I looked at her and said, "Mom, did you get lost?"

"Are you kidding?" she said. "I sure did! I went all the way to Jackson, where the state prison is."

Feeling somewhat more relaxed, she watched as my friends put all my belongings in the car and bid me goodbye. When we got home, my father asked her, "Did you write a check?"

"Of course," she said. "I was almost out of gas."

He nodded and explained that the gas station attendant had phoned and told him that a Helen Pompeian had written a check in the checkbook of someone else named Sharon. In her haste, my mother had somehow gotten hold of my sister's checkbook. All that had mattered to her was to get to her son, and bring him home.

*

It was obvious to everyone that I was sick, but the doctors at the hospital in Birmingham were conflicted as to how to move forward. My mother had met a doctor at Ford Hospital in Detroit, and wanted to transfer me to that facility. "Go ahead," one of the doctors told her. "But I think you're making a terrible mistake by taking him anywhere right now. He's a very sick boy."

At Ford Hospital I was given a series of tests and after a thorough examination it was decided that I needed to be put on peritoneal dialysis. The first night was a painful and difficult one. A dialysate solution was pumped into my abdominal cavity and then removed, in a procedure that cleansed impurities from my blood. The procedure was done without anesthetic. As the painful and difficult process wore on through the night, I looked up at my mother and said, "Mom, I'm so cold…"

I could feel my head moving from side to side, but I had no way to control my movements, no matter how hard I tried. Panicked, I said, "I can't stop my head from moving."

My mother raced down the hallway to the nurses' station. "My son needs help!" she cried, frantic.

Minutes ticked by with agonizing slowness as my mother waited with me in my room. My condition was worsening. It felt as though my body was freezing from the inside out. Again my mother ran down the hall and demanded the nurse get a doctor.

It seemed like hours before a nurse and doctor arrived. My dialysate solution wasn't circulating properly and rather than getting the warm solution I was getting it cold. One of the medications I was being given to control my nausea, Compazine, was causing my involuntary head movements.

In all my years of pain and precarious health, I couldn't remember feeling more terrified. Suddenly, I had a flash of inspiration. I looked up at my mother and said, "Please call the Letos. I want to see Sam as soon as possible."

My mother could see from the look in my eyes how important it was to me to see our friends once again. But she didn't have their unlisted number with her. She pleaded with the operator, explaining the danger I was in and how important it was that she get a message to Sam, who thought of me as his "fourth son." But the operator was unmoved, refusing even to call the Letos to ask them to call her back. Sadly, she returned to my room.

Then, just a short while later, the Letos arrived—as if miraculously. When I saw them I was filled with gratitude as I exclaimed, "Oh, Sam!"

My mother asked them how they happened to be at Ford Hospital. Sam told her that he and Mary had a strong feeling that I needed them, so they tried to call me at home. When they got no answer, they began calling area hospitals, and finally found us at Ford.

The Letos' visits continued for almost a week, and lifted my spirits immeasurably. My condition improved slowly, until Ford doctors made arrangements for me to visit Mt. Carmel Mercy Hospital in Detroit, which had a highly specialized kidney unit. In early 1970, this facility was the area's only dialysis center.

On our first visit to this hospital, we were directed to the kidney unit lobby. In this small room we were surprised to find many patients and their family members, wearing worried expressions. We had expected that I would begin receiving regular treatments immediately. However, we soon learned that I was actually one of many patients who would be evaluated to determine who among us would derive the most benefit from the use of one of the limited number of available kidney machines. I would have to submit to yet another in the series of tests that seemed to punctuate my life.

Unfortunately, this experience wasn't unique for the time. There were so few dialysis centers and machines in the United States that many people who needed them had to be turned away.

After several anxious days of worrying, I was selected. My dialysis treatment was administered three days a week for six hours a day using a Travenol artificial kidney machine. The large and unwieldy device, with its motors, gears, buttons, and metal drum, seemed to resemble a large washing machine. (In fact Willem Kolff, who created the original artificial kidney machine, actually used Maytag washing machine parts in its construction. When Maytag found out they asked him to stop. They were afraid of having to assume legal liability if anyone died while using one.)

The delicate state of my veins meant that using a needle to collect my blood was impossible. For this reason a Quinton-Scribner Teflon shunt was implanted—one end into a vein and the other end into an artery. This was a painful, time-consuming process that left horrifying scars on my arms. My mother was amazed at my ability to endure this litany of pain, as well as the serious infections I contracted.

The blood left my body to be collected in the Travenol machine, which removed the impurities that my almost completely nonfunctioning kidneys couldn't, and then the blood was returned. The shunt was permanent, but at some point it would clot off. If it couldn't be de-clotted, it needed to be replaced in another location.

For three months, my parents and I made the thirty-mile journey from our home in Birmingham to Mt. Carmel. The treatments cost a great deal of money, and there was no way of knowing how long they would be required. Perhaps even more worrisome was the fact that we had absolutely no confidence in Mt. Carmel Mercy's doctors. In addition to their negative attitude regarding my prognosis, their shunt implantation had caused serious damage to the skin and muscle of my arms—damage that would affect my arms for the rest of my life.

Finally, we were able to continue my treatments at home.

Over the course of his life, my father had run a number of businesses. A pool hall was shut down by the city, but he turned it into a restaurant called Pompeian's Chicken Roost. Behind this storefront he ran a boarding house for elderly men. The city bought the property, and my father used the money to purchase two other boarding houses. These helped pay most of our family's bills—but we didn't have health insurance.

My mother and father were both active with the veterans service group AMVETS, participating in fundraising drives and garage sales. Everyone in our tight-knit community knew about my health problems. It was during an AMVETS event that someone approached my father and told him that General Motors was hiring, and offering excellent health insurance benefits. My father applied for and got a job as a welder, a trade he'd had some experience with. This job not only paid for my healthcare, it also allowed him to work at night and help with my dialysis during the day.

My father committed himself to learning every detail of how to use the Travenol machine so that he could safely dialyze me at home. For her part, my mother was in charge of preparing the equipment, which included cleaning and sterilizing every component of the machine. In addition, she had to ensure the dialysate solution was kept at the proper temperature.

The process combined tedium with anxiety. With the Travenol machine in my bedroom, I would lie on my own bed for six hours per day three times a week, feeling my blood flowing through me, leaving my body, while the machine hummed and clanged. The lines between my hospital life and my home life would blur in my mind as I waited for the cycle to complete.

My entire world revolved around the dialysis machine. The process left me feeling run down and groggy—it was difficult to concentrate on matters that weren't related to my health, or the routine that kept me alive. Even so, I was inspired by the fact that God was watching over me, giving me the courage and support I needed.

Slowly, my condition improved and I felt my strength returning. By September 1970, I seemed well enough to begin another semester at college. Because I needed to stay close to home I started at Oakland Community College, which was about 30 miles away in Farmington, Michigan. I would dialyze Tuesday, Thursday, and Saturday. Typically, by the next day I felt well enough to engage in my "normal" activities, allowing me to attend classes at Oakland Community College on Monday, Wednesday, and Friday.

My course selection reflected a desire to study law and business administration. I made new friends and enjoyed my classes, earning the title of "Superior Student."

My at-home treatments lasted for two years. In that time, my family and I were blessed to have so much support from friends and family, including those people I'd met at the beginning of my illness.

As time wore on, my mother was able to accept an invitation from the National Kidney Foundation to chair a committee to organize a fund drive. This represented a great opportunity for us to help raise money for and awareness of kidney disease. My mother recruited friends, neighbors, and family members to help sell innumerable bags of Halloween candy that had been delivered by the Foundation. Even though I couldn't sell door-to-door, I was able to get involved as the fundraiser's treasurer. Our efforts constituted Birmingham's first National Kidney Foundation fundraiser ever, and became one of the state's top-ten fundraisers of the year.

All along, my mother had kept in touch with the doctors at Mayo.

In 1954 Dr. Joseph Murray of Boston's Peter Bent Brigham Hospital transplanted a kidney from Ronald Herrick into his brother Richard, who was suffering with kidney disease. In the case of this first successful transplant rejection wasn't an issue, given the fact that Richard and Ronald were identical twins—Richard's immune system saw Ronald's kidney as indistinguishable from his own. Several other transplants were performed between identical twin patients, but there were still many obstacles to overcome before transplants could become commonplace. It took years of advances in matching of blood and tissue types, as well as immunosuppression techniques. Throughout the 1960s, researchers made miraculous breakthroughs with immunosuppressive drugs, lowering the dangers associated with transplants.

Finally, in the spring of 1972, the Mayo Clinic contacted us and told us that transplant technology had progressed to a point where they believed that I could benefit. I needed to go to the Mayo Clinic to complete a donor workup, to ensure I was well enough to have a transplant and to determine if there was a compatible donor in our immediate family. In August my mother, my sister Sharon, Sharon's two year-old son Paul, and I drove to Rochester.

I felt blessed to hear my mother and sister arguing over which of them would be the better match. I had two willing donors! I understood just how lucky I was to be part of such a loving family, with people who would volunteer to give up a part of their body for me.

In those early days of organ transplantation, the blood types of donors and recipients needed to be the same. Sharon, who shared the same blood type as our father, was eliminated as a potential donor. My mother and I shared the same type, so we began our transplant journey.

Sharon had her own emotional turmoil to deal with. Her marriage, which had started with so much promise, had collapsed. She devoted herself fully to helping me and our mother, assuming full responsibility for finding suitable living arrangements. Staying in hotels and eating in restaurants contributed to our financial burden and our stress. It took about two weeks for Sharon to find us an apartment, which helped to add a sense of stability to our hectic lives.

In the meantime, I was still on my regular dialysis schedule. I was one of several patients who were close enough together in the dialysis room that we could all become acquainted. As hopeful as we were about our treatments, there was often a feeling of tension in the room. I tried to amuse them with jokes as well as stories from my own life. I kept the stories light, putting an amusing and hopeful spin on what were very difficult experiences. If the nurses who were dialyzing patients had names that were in songs, I would sing that song to them—for instance, one nurse named Sheila was treated to my rendition of Tommy Roe's 1962 hit "Sheila." I'm not sure if my singing made her feel "so doggone happy," but I hope so.

Even when suffering through the most painful and difficult

periods of illness, my joy for life never wavered. I was usually seated near the dialysis center entrance where I would act as an unofficial "greeter." In fact, my presence was so uplifting that doctors would seat me next to patients who were depressed and having the most difficulty coping. I'm happy to be able to say that, in some small way, my companionship gave them some comfort. Before long I had the other patients sharing their own stories and feeling far more upbeat about their situation. Doctors would also bring me a telephone so I could call friends and family members.

I also convinced my mother to bring food in every once in a while, as a change of pace from our normal gastronomic fare. She loved being part of what would grow to become if not quite a party, then a much-needed variation on our daily routine. At this time Mayo allowed patients to eat anything they wanted while they were dialyzing, so she took orders for pizza, ham dinners, and Chinese food. When patients were off dialysis our diet was so restrictive that many of us actually *looked forward* to dialysis!

Despite our hope for the future, the drastic changes in our lives were taking an emotional toll on all of us. We'd moved to a new city, leaving behind our family and an established circle of friends, and there was still a great deal of uncertainty regarding my condition.

I believed that there were three major factors that contributed to my ability to cope with all my medical challenges. The first was my immediate family—my parents, Sharon, and nephew Paul. Second was my faith in God. And third was my Armenian heritage.

The Armenian people had to endure significant brutality and horrible tortures at the hands of the Turks, and my family had lived through these horrors. My paternal grandmother escaped Turkey with my father, but not before my father, who was five years old at the time, witnessed the brutal murder of his father at the hands of the Turks. My father's twin siblings starved and died on the death march. My father helped his mother bury the twins.

As the transplant date approached, my mother was plagued by terrifying nightmares of our family's ordeal. She saw herself suffering the agony of the massacres as her parents had. Somehow her parents, who hadn't known each other at the time, found a miraculous means of escape. Her mother, sixteen years of age, as well as several Armenian friends, had lived together in a home that my mother's grandparents had owned. In terror, they were able to make the difficult journey through Constantinople, and found their way to a ship to travel to the United States. Arriving at Ellis Island, she was met by relatives who took her to Pontiac, where she would meet her future husband.

Every night, my mother relived these horrors. There were nights when she feared going to sleep. The dreams were a manifestation of the anxiety she endured in the face of my health challenges. For my sake she tried to stay focused on the positive. But subconsciously she couldn't help but connect our family's suffering in the past with my own suffering in the present.

*

Finally it was time to begin the series of surgical procedures that would culminate in the kidney transplant. The doctors were pleased with the progress that I was showing. My strength was returning and my health was improving, so I was scheduled to undergo a nephrectomy (removal of the kidneys), appendectomy, and the removal of the spleen on September 15, 1972. The transplant would follow soon thereafter.

These procedures went well, but I lost a lot of strength and my blood pressure dropped. One morning, a nurse asked me to get out of bed so that I could be weighed.

"I'm not sure I can make it out of bed," I said. I felt exhausted.

"I'll help you," the nurse said. She helped me to stand, but as we were making our way to the scales, I felt the room begin to spin—then suddenly I hit the floor with a loud thud, my incision splitting open.

I was rushed in for emergency surgery to repair the damage, but my situation took a bleak turn. More major surgeries followed; with each procedure the surgeons lost confidence in my body's recuperative abilities. In addition to delayed healing, I suffered from pneumonia and pancreatitis.

One terrible night, my mother was told that she might want to call the family in. The doctors weren't sure I was going to make it.

The months of September, October, and November were spent in the hospital. My mother wondered every day if this would be my last, and her relentless fear exacted a painful toll. In order to help keep our spirits up, the family made Thanksgiving plans which included inviting our dialysis friends who were in Rochester without family. I was allowed to leave the hospital for that day. My mother prepared a large, traditional meal, and all of us felt blessed to have this special time together.

*

I was released from the hospital in December. I needed to build my strength up before the transplant. Now we were in a holding pattern of sorts; so much depended on my body and its ability to heal. My family did everything they could to help, looking forward to the new year with hope and an abiding faith that God would make 1973 our best year since before my medical troubles began.

Throughout everything I, my mother, Sharon, and Paul grew to love the city of Rochester. Like us, thousands of people journeyed from all over the world to have major health problems addressed at the Mayo Clinic. The more we learned, the more this city of just under 54,000 residents felt like home.

On New Year's Day 1973, we told our family and friends that we'd decided to remain in Rochester. Sharon found us a permanent living space a short time later.

I would go to the YMCA and walk around the track to build my stamina. Slowly, my strength improved. I continued making my regular three-times-a-week dialysis trips to the Mayo Clinic, showing amazing progress given everything I'd been through in the previous six months.

In 1973, there was no organized support program for transplant patients. Doctors and nurses did their best to understand what we were going through. Of course they were able to provide medical information, but they had no firsthand knowledge of the peculiar mixture of fear, anxiety, and hope that patients and loved ones experienced, and what challenges they faced in the future.

Previous transplant patients were an invaluable resource, providing information and support. Following their operations, they'd return for follow up exams and blood work. While waiting for the doctors to arrive with their results, they would spend time with current transplant patients. For me and so many others, these visits provided a reason to believe that a bright future awaited us. Seeing people who were out of the hospital and doing well showed us that we too had a great deal to look forward to.
*

One cold midwinter's day, while Paul was wheeling me down the hall following another round of dialysis, two of my doctors, William J. Johnson and Richard D. Wagoner, stopped us in the hall, smiling.

"Have you heard the good news, Mrs. Pompeian?" Dr. Johnson asked.

"We haven't heard anything special," my mother said, taken aback.

"We've scheduled April twenty-sixth for Edward's transplant," he said.

This was the happy news we'd been waiting so long to hear.

My mother was overwhelmed. A wave of relief washed over her and she began to cry. Our prayers had finally brought the blessed day within sight. After nearly eleven dreadful years of illness, God had seen us through. April twenty-sixth was a date full of promise and hope—not only was it the day of my transplant, it was Paul's birthday. It would also serve as a birthday, of sorts, for me. The start of my new life.

My graduation picture

Chapter Five: A brand new life

Our faith was rewarded and our perseverance paid off. Mary and I organized a caring group of people who dedicated themselves to the large and difficult challenges that lay ahead. Area hotels and motels volunteered furniture. We found people to clean, repair, paint, and provide other services as needed. Brentwood Motor Inn donated housekeeping services for a year, and the desk clerks handled reservations until other arrangements could be made. Numerous people donated household items and other supplies. As word spread, more donations came in, with places like Slumberland donating new mattresses. Two college students named Brenda and Kelly volunteered their time in exchange for a sleeping room.

Anyone who had a transplant or who was being considered for transplant was welcome to reside at the Gift of Life Transplant House. However, it was necessary to establish a system to determine who would need financial assistance or free housing. Mayo Clinic Social Services generously took on that responsibility. Thanks to the tireless efforts of many dedicated volunteers, transplant patients would be able to keep the focus on their own health requirements, without having to worry about housing.

The challenges they faced were stressful enough.

Before a living donor transplant surgery can take place, both the donor and recipient must undergo a thorough psychiatric examination. It's important to determine that the donor's offer is being made because of a true desire to give the patient a chance at better health—that their motivation is kindness, not a sense of guilt or pressure to do the "right thing."

My mother, motivated solely by her compassionate love for me, "passed" the examination. But as the date of the transplant drew closer she began to experience new, terrifying nightmares that revolved around the death of her loving and caring father. When she was eight years old, he had been killed in a terrible train accident. In her dream, she saw herself as a teenager, staring at the gruesome results of the disaster and feeling that she was somehow at fault.

She struggled to understand what connected this tragic incident from her childhood with her current situation all these years later, when she was a mother and a grandmother. She did know why she missed her father, and wished that he could have been there with her, to give her comfort when she felt so much stress.

This dream recurred until one night just before the date of the transplant, when it was replaced by what she would later call a vision. She and I were sleeping in the same room when God walked between our beds, His flowing robes touching us softly from our heads to our toes. He lifted His arms, offering us His blessing.

Upon awakening, my mother came to my bedside and told me about the vision. "It's a message," she said, "that everything will be all right."

Barely awake, I replied, "I hope so, Mom."

*

The day before the transplant, my mother checked in for preliminary tests, and remained in the hospital overnight for an arteriogram dye test. This procedure involved injecting dye into the aorta, helping to give the doctors a complete picture of the function and arterial anatomy of the kidneys. It was determined that both her kidneys were functioning normally, and she could live a healthy life with one kidney.

The day of the transplant, the two of us were kept in separate rooms. Although we didn't see one another, we shared a feeling that could almost be described as calmness. Yes, this was a huge event in our lives—it was to be a defining moment for both of us—but we had complete confidence in our surgical team, headed by Drs. John E. Woods and Franklin J. Leary.

We were taken to the operating rooms independently, neither of us knowing exactly what to expect, but filled with hope for the future.

*

By degrees, my mother could feel herself regaining consciousness. Her eyes, heavy with sleep, opened slowly, and she was confronted by the harsh glare of the fluorescent lights. For a moment she wasn't sure where she was, then suddenly, the word *Transplant* entered her thoughts. Of course. *Edward.*

What are we waiting for? When is the operation going to begin?

She realized someone was calling her name. That's what had awakened her.

Awakened her? Had she been asleep?

She must have been speaking, because a voice was answering her:

"It's done, Helen. You and Edward have both come through with flying colors."

She now realized that she was in a recovery room. Not long after she'd awakened, Sharon entered the room, barely able to contain her excitement. Ten minutes after the graft of the new kidney and the transplant were completed, I had begun to void. The two of them tearfully thanked God for blessing them, after so many years of painful and terrifying struggle.

*

Immediately following the transplant, everything changed for me. It was as if I had suddenly opened the door to a brand new life. That very day I was allowed to eat solid food, and even started walking. I was overcome with gratitude for my mother for making this sacrifice, the family and friends who had supported us for so long, the skilled doctors who'd performed the transplant so successfully, and God for blessing us with strength and love.

I spent three weeks in the hospital, after which I began to experience those things I'd missed out on when my life had revolved around the thrice-weekly dialysis regimen. Now the only restrictions on my diet were alcohol and smoking.[1] I definitely made up for lost time, eating and drinking a lot of everything, without carefully measuring the amount of protein or sodium I was taking in. I enjoyed foods with real *flavor*. Most importantly, I seemed to have boundless energy and renewed hope for the future.

There were relatively minor medical issues to deal with after the procedure. Elevated calcium levels required vitamin D treatments, and the removal of seventy-five percent of my parathyroid glands. A lymphocele (a buildup of lymphatic fluid) required surgery. In 1976 I was involved in an automobile accident in which my wrist was broken. But for the most part, I had entered a completely new phase of life. I was often fond of saying, "So far in life since my illness began, everything that is good has happened to me in Rochester."

But my brand new life didn't mean I'd be saying goodbye to

---

[1] In the early days of transplant surgery, patients were essentially told not to smoke or drink, but that just about everything else was okay. Today's transplant patients are given a much more rigorous health-maintenance regimen.

the Mayo Clinic or the transplant community that had been so important to me. I was determined to share my blessings with others.

*

The world was now open to me like it had never been before, and I wanted to go back to college. I still didn't have my degree, and my illness had made it impossible to work.

After my transplant in April 1973, I started visiting new transplants on a daily basis. I would continue to do so up until our first child was born in 1983. One of the people I met during one of those visits was John Kling, a doctor of psychology who was a teacher at St. Theresa's College in Winona, Minnesota. He told me that St. Theresa's, which had been an all-girl school, would begin accepting male students in the fall of 1973.

I applied and was accepted, and began taking science courses in preparation for becoming a microbiologist. I definitely enjoyed being the only male student at that time. My studies at St. Theresa's were supplemented with courses at Rochester Community College. I took an efficiency apartment, driving back and forth between Rochester and Winona.

Sharon was also a student at the community college, and the two of us had a few classes together. Sharon had taken an active role in my care early on. She'd intended on helping me dialyze once we arrived in Rochester, but when we made the move the talk turned to transplant preparation. A surgeon at Methodist taught her how to administer my Solu-Medrol IV—this was the first tentative step in her nursing career, and her classes were the next step. She would go on to become a registered nurse, taking a job at Saint Marys Hospital.

I was hired at Mayo's microbiology lab for weekends and summer when classes weren't in session. However, when my doctors discovered I was working in the lab, they showed a great deal of concern over my career choice. My immunosuppression meant I was vulnerable to infection and communicable diseases. The microbiology lab, therefore, was potentially a very dangerous environment for me. Mayo had their infectious disease specialists monitor my work. In the end it was decided that it would be best if I selected a different vocation.

*

The strain of studying at two different schools and the back-and-forth driving took their toll, and I became sick again. Although this was a mild illness compared to what I had dealt with in the past, it forced me to put an end to my studies.

It was 1975. I was now twenty-three years old with little education, no training, and no career prospects. I had no clue what the future held, which was both exciting and terrifying. But I knew that by trusting God I'd find my true calling.

One day I was searching the newspaper classified section, looking for suitable employment. I saw an ad for a real estate company called Wendland and Robertson Realtors. They were looking for agents—no experience necessary.

Wendland and Robertson Realtors was one of the first real estate firms in the Rochester area. Partners Vern Wendland and Robert "Robbie" Robertson had been involved in many real estate transactions during their long careers. I was one of twenty-five new agents brought on to help the company jumpstart their sales.

Almost immediately I knew I was on the right professional path.

For our first year, Wendland and Robertson insisted all new agents sell residential real estate, before venturing into commercial and investment sales. What I discovered was that residential buyers are often a fickle lot, telling me they wanted one thing, then settling on something completely different. Moreover, most of the people that I met were more interested in buying income property than a home for their family.

While I got to meet a lot of "wheelers and dealers" of Rochester real estate, it was a bumpy first year for me. I sold a total of two homes: one to a former co-worker in the microbiology lab, and one to my mother.

This wasn't exactly an illustrious beginning.

Perhaps the most important event in my first year selling real estate was meeting Daryl Engelhardt. Daryl was an IBM engineer who would become one of my first clients, a lifelong friend, and my real estate partner for over thirty-three years.

It wasn't until the second year that my real estate career finally began to take off. I sold over two million dollars in income property for Wendland and Robertson, then in 1977 Daryl and I established our own practice, Pompeian Engelhardt McQuarry Realty. When McQuarry left the following year, Daryl and I formed a new entity, Reality Growth, Inc.

Now I felt I was truly on my way; all the anxiety I'd felt about my future was gone. I was good at my job, and I enjoyed it, but a major turning point in my career came when Nyal Bishoff, a friend from Michigan who'd also gone into real estate, told me about the Certified Commercial Investment Member (CCIM) designation that I could obtain through the National Association of Realtors. I started taking courses in 1978 and completed all the coursework and examinations in Miami Beach in 1981. The process was difficult but was beneficial in making me the most knowledgeable realty professional I could be, so I could assist my clients with their investment choices and consult with business owners on the value of their business.

Years later, I ran into a man called Henry DeCook, who'd started as an agent trainee at Wendland and Robertson the same year I had. Henry told me that of the twenty-five agents trained, I was voted the least likely to succeed. He then laughed and told me, "You're the only one that ever made it!"

God took care of me, guiding me on the right path. I was careful to listen, and my experience in commercial real estate was crucial to my establishment of the Gift of Life Transplant House.

*

My mother also continued to work to improve the lives of transplant patients. Remembering her success with the candy sale back in Pontiac, she organized several groups of women in small towns around Rochester, in particular Byron. Together they raised a surprising amount of money by selling candy door-to-door, and in shopping malls and other businesses.

These achievements, as well as the desire to help others who were going through the same difficulties that she and I had endured, inspired her to do even more. She talked about it with anyone who would listen. Her idea was to try to get a celebrity to chair an Upper Midwest fundraising event.

Finally, my aunt Janet's in-laws, Helen and Edward Mardigian, suggested that my mother extend an invitation to Mike Connors, star of the hit TV show *Mannix*. As it turned out, he was a friend of theirs. They suggested that my mother send him a brief letter outlining my story as well as some information about the work of the National Kidney Foundation.

To her surprise and delight, Mr. Connors accepted the invitation. Now she had to ensure everything was organized for Mr. Connors' arrival, and take care of the all the event logistics.

On March 25, 1977, a small group gathered at the Minneapolis airport to greet the actor. My mother, the National Kidney

Foundation chairman, and a few others took him by limousine to his hotel. That evening, they held a reception at the home of Dr. John Najarian, the chief transplant surgeon at the University of Minnesota hospitals. The guest list included about sixty-five Armenians, including Mr. Connors himself. A lavish Armenian buffet was served, and there was music provided by two famous musicians, violinists Arsham Ohanessian and Henry Gregorian.

The following evening a testimonial dinner was held at the Marquette Inn in Minneapolis. Dr. Najarian introduced Mr. Connors as the honorary chairman of the drive. My mother had a grand time sitting beside Mr. Connors! In addition to the work they did raising funds for kidney research, she was impressed to learn of Mr. Connors' interest in Armenian history and his knowledge of the Armenian massacres which claimed the lives of more than a million Armenians.

Throughout her life, my mother remained steadfast in her belief that these horrible atrocities should never be forgotten. Not just because of her own heritage, but to prevent such horrors ever happening again. She dedicated herself to preserving her own family history, maintaining copious notes and collecting the stories of those from her past who had inspired her throughout her life, and whose blood now coursed through her veins.

Chapter Six: Lifelong connections

Since moving to Rochester, my social life had revolved around the Mayo Clinic. The doctors, nurses, and my fellow patients served as an extended family, and I developed lifelong friendships with many of them. After my transplant, I continued to visit the clinic. I felt good knowing that I was helping people through what I knew to be a difficult and anxious process. I answered questions about surgery, and if there was a donor question, my mother was always happy to provide her own insights. Together, we became the go-to information source for patients and their families. Maybe it was because I was "one of them," a transplant club member, but the patients felt at ease with both me and my mother.

I told them to make sure to always follow the advice of the doctors and nurses, and to also pray to God for His hand in healing them.

In a sense I was building a community. I drew inspiration and strength from these contacts. In addition, I was meeting people who would have a major impact on my life and on the Gift of Life Transplant House.

Among those I met was attorney Mark Torgrimson. One day while making my transplant rounds, I entered Mark's room just after his kidney transplant surgery was complete. Returning to consciousness he struggled to open his eyes and saw my face, silhouetted by the light of the room's florescent bulbs. As he would later put it, "The first thing I remember seeing was the round face of Ed Pompeian staring down at me, and I thought I had died!"

It was Mark that I consulted when I set up the entity that would administer the transplant house. Mark and his law firm donated important legal assistance. He was also the one who came up with the name "Gift of Life."

Another lifelong friend was Norm Gillette. We met while I was waiting for blood test results at Mayo building W17. We struck up a conversation and later met for breakfast. When I conceived of the transplant house, Norm was one of the first people I told about it. He owned a Pepsi franchise, and in addition to moral support, he generously provided much-needed financial assistance when the Gift of Life Transplant House was founded, and throughout its expansion.

Without him, I'm not sure the Gift of Life Transplant House would even exist.

Not only that, Norm would become my best friend and would often go on vacations with my family. Once during a phone conversation, I told Norm that my wife and I were going on a cruise to celebrate our fifteenth wedding anniversary. Norm immediately asked, "Can I come along?" Norm's presence turned out to be a welcome distraction when my wife and I were suffering from a severe bout of seasickness.

Eventually people took to calling us brothers. In a way we were transplant brothers, I suppose. Our personal friendship was difficult for some to understand. We were so close we could discuss anything—and I mean *anything*—with each other. He had an amazing love of life and a wonderful sense of humor, supplying me with many stories and jokes. He was always willing to help anyone, at any time, especially transplant patients.

When Norm was diagnosed with terminal cancer he chose me to be in charge of his final medical decisions, and included me in his estate planning. Making the decision regarding his health directive was one of the most difficult things I have ever had to do. I'd faced many grave situations in my own life, and I thought I was strong enough to handle it. But when the time came it was a painful emotional challenge. I spent a lot of time praying for God's help and guidance, and thankfully I was able to carry out his wishes.

Although he passed away in 2003, his family has continued providing generous support for the Gift of Life Transplant House. He also created the Norman L. Gillett Jr. Charitable Trust Fund so that I could continue his good works, to provide funding to non-profits that Norm would have supported.

*

Another friend was Elic Coombs. Because Elic had an infection in his mouth, he couldn't be on the transplant wing. After visiting the other patients, I would then go up to Elic's room.

During one visit in November, 1979, I was relaxing on Elic's bed, while Elic sat on a nearby chair. The two of us were talking and laughing, preparing for a quick trip outside the hospital. This was in the days before outpatient care, and Elic was in the hospital on a ten-day antibiotic course; after his treatment he was allowed to leave the hospital, provided he returned by midnight.

As Elic was getting ready to leave, a nurse walked into the room, carrying the heparin flush for Elic's IV. I had seen her before, but this was my first opportunity to talk to her. I was struck by her friendly smile and spirit that seemed to shine through her. She stopped short and in a playful tone asked, "Just who's the patient here?"

"Well, it depends on what's in that syringe!" I replied.

As Elic and I were preparing to leave the nurse told me, "You know, it's really not fair that you guys get to go out and have fun, while the rest of us are stuck here. The least you can do is bring us back some popcorn!"

Before returning to the hospital that night, I stopped at a grocery store and asked the manager for all the popcorn they had. I filled a large garbage bag—which was nearly as tall as I was—with four dollars' worth of popcorn and returned to the hospital, leaving it for her at the nurse's station.

Her name was Jayne Ann Diercks. I was smitten, to say the least.

Jayne's mother had been a nurse, and Jayne herself had known that she wanted to follow in her mother's footsteps since high school in Red Wing, Minnesota. She took a test that showed she had a high aptitude for the work, and got a scholarship from the local chapter of the hospital auxiliary volunteers known as the Pink Ladies. She honed her skills at a vocational school, then in December 1976 she got a job in the Methodist Hospital gynecologic surgical unit. In the fall of 1979 she moved to general surgery.

I confided to Elic, "You know, that's the kind of girl I wouldn't mind marrying."

Elic scoffed. "Oh, you don't want to marry her," he said.

"Why not?"

"She's too friendly!"

Happily I decided to ignore Elic's questionable advice, and called her for a date the next day.

She gulped. She didn't want to say no, but she already had plans: "I can't tomorrow. I have to pick up my mother at the airport." Then she said something that she herself found surprising: "Could I get a rain check?"

She was surprised because she wasn't entirely sure what the phrase meant. It was as if God had given her a push, telling her what to ask.

"All right," I said. "Let's pick another time now."

Just as God had guided me through so many trials to get me to this moment, He now spoke to Jayne, telling her that she should accept my offer.

"You can set the date," I prodded, when she still hadn't answered me.

Jayne agreed to meet me for lunch in two days. I picked her up at the YMCA where she often worked out. Our first date was at a Rochester institution called Michael's Restaurant. Located on South Broadway just a few blocks from the Mayo Clinic, Michael's had been a favorite and a destination spot for visitors to the city, since 1951.[2]

From then on, we were rarely ever apart. I continued my courtship with more dates and romantic gestures such as leaving notes on the windshield of Jayne's Dodge Colt. We were engaged in April 1980, and married on September 27, 1980.

In attendance were many of the doctors and nurses who'd helped ensure my survival, as well as other transplant recipients—three of whom served as my groomsmen. The large wedding was a joyous affirmation of life and included my family from Michigan, Jayne's family, and all of our friends from all over the world. The daughter of one of my surgeons sang. All told, about 300 people attended.

The ceremony was officiated by Rev. J. Charles "Chuck" Parker, a close friend of mine and another transplant recipient. But he and I weren't always so close—in fact when we first met, Chuck couldn't stand me!

Back when I was dialyzing at the Mayo Clinic I was of course known for my upbeat, loquacious attitude. One day, Chuck was seated next to me, and I tried again and again to strike up a conversation with him. Each time Chuck politely declined. He found my antics to be annoying, and he even asked not to be placed beside me in the future.

But I remained undeterred and eventually we became such great friends that when he had an operation on his nose at the same time I was having my wisdom teeth pulled, we arranged to be placed in the same hospital room. Following our procedures,

---

[2] It would go on to become extremely important to our family. We'd return for special occasions including Christmas, birthdays, proms, and more. Jayne and I and our children would sometimes even sit at the booth where we'd had our first date. We continued to frequent Michael's until its closing on January 1, 2015 as part of the Mayo Destination Medical Center downtown redevelopment project.

Chuck decided he wanted to get out of town so he wouldn't have to talk about his surgery. We settled on a trip to Las Vegas, and what a pair we were: Him with his bandaged nose and me with my swollen cheeks.

Chuck loved to tell the story of that trip because, as he put it, Las Vegas was where I became a man. No, it's not what you might be thinking. While we were seeing the sights we wandered into Circus Circus where a couple of attractive young women were imploring naïve Midwestern boys to spend $150 on watches that were worth, at most, $10. I took the bait. Back at the hotel that night I tossed and turned, berating myself for my gullibility. I told Chuck I was determined to get my money back.

The next day we went back to Circus Circus and I walked straight up to the salesman who was seated at a raised table that resembled a judge's podium. In front of all the other "marks," I slammed my overpriced trinket on the table and loudly proclaimed my intention to get my money back. The salesman informed me that there were no refunds and then asked me, "Just who do you think you are, anyway?" I told him I was an attorney who was willing to work for free to prove that he was practicing fraud and misrepresentation.

"Give this man his money and get him out of here!" the salesman shouted.

Chuck beamed with pride, and never forgot our trip to Las Vegas.

*

Jayne and I spent our honeymoon in Medellin, Colombia. It was my third visit to the area. One of my closest transplant friends was Luis Uribe. Luis had invited me to visit him at his home for the first time in 1976, just after his transplant at Mayo. It was an exciting time for me, because I was enjoying a relatively healthy period, and was happy for the opportunity to experience travel to an exotic location.

At one point during my first trip, Luis's wife Angela and I joined Luis at the City Hall in Guarne, Colombia. There was a reception and dinner, with dozens of dignitaries and local government officials. Everyone stood, faced me, and raised their champagne glasses. They began to speak in Spanish.

I nodded and smiled politely. Then I turned to Angela and said, "What are they saying?"

Angela smiled back and said, "Just play along. Luis told

everyone that you were the mayor of Rochester, and they're toasting you."

As the "mayor of Rochester," I was treated to a ride in a car with the queen, and a private audience with the Medellin chief of police. We were also invited to the Policeman's Ball and a bullfight.

Years later, Luis returned to Rochester for follow up treatment. He stayed with my family, and I arranged a surprise of my own. Luis awoke one morning to find a stranger in the house, standing next to me. I couldn't help myself—I had a big smile on my face. "Luis," I said, "I have a real treat for you."

"Oh?"

I turned toward the other man and said, "Let me introduce you to the *actual* mayor of Rochester!"

Luis laughed long and hearty. He loved to play tricks, and now I had tricked him.

Jayne and I stayed in Luis's condo, and had a great time. Throughout our lives, the two of us would pay visits to transplant recipients around the world, including Italy, Mexico, and several states. These people are part of our extended family, sharing a common bond as recipients of the precious gift of life.

Just as my mother and I had done before, I continued to invite fellow transplant recipients over to our home for meals or to stay on the couch in our guest room while they were in town. Members of the "transplant club" were part of our family, and if there wasn't enough room at the transplant house or one of the hotels, we always opened our home to them.

Jayne knew she wasn't just marrying me—she was marrying into my dream. It was fundamental to who I was, and she was happy to be able to provide support and encouragement.

My condition interrupted the normal trajectory of my life, creating a new path for me to follow. The connections that others make in school and their neighborhoods, I made in hospital hallways and in dialysis units. My closest friends were those I met on my long and arduous transplant journey—from the Letos at Cottage Hospital in Grosse Point, Michigan, to the small Korean girl at Saint Marys Hospital, to Norm Gillette, to the nurse who would become my wife.

*

Before proposing, I told Jayne that because of my ongoing health issues, it was unlikely that I'd ever be able to father children. I had been tested at Mayo and the doctor told me I had a very low sperm count. (He discussed artificial insemination options and stated, "Don't be concerned about birth control!"— famous last words!) Jayne was confident that God would provide us with the strength and guidance we needed to face any obstacle. And she had an unwavering faith that we were meant to be parents.

Two years later, we were relieved when Jayne discovered she was pregnant. That first unlikely pregnancy was followed by three more in rapid succession. Each of our four children—Edward Paul, Aaron, Nick, and Adrienne—is a living, breathing reminder of the power of God in our lives.

*

Transplant patients required once-a-year follow up examinations, so I organized a yearly reunion dinner. Everyone agreed to plan their registration times early enough that they could meet at roughly the same time each year. The chosen date was the first Sunday after Easter. It was wonderful to maintain this connection, build a support system, and catch up with fellow transplant recipients. This gathering was a precursor of the annual transplant picnic that continues to this day.

But I knew there was even more that I could do.

I had firsthand knowledge of just how difficult it was for transplant patients and their families to find affordable temporary housing when they came to the clinic for their preliminary care, the transplant procedure, and follow up care. They needed to be near the clinic immediately before the procedure and for weeks and sometimes months after. This usually meant living in motels and hotels and eating out in restaurants, all while maintaining their residence back home. When I came back to the clinic for checkups and to meet with current transplant patients, they invariably asked me if I knew of a place to stay with good accommodations at reasonable prices.

In 1976 Daryl and I purchased the Regency West Apartments, which was located just a few blocks from the clinic. Although it wasn't a large complex, we reserved five apartments for kidney patients, charging very little while making occupants as comfortable as possible. These five units represented the first tentative steps toward what would become the Gift of Life Transplant House, and when we had to sell the building four years later the buyer, Methodist Hospital, complied with our request to continue to use those five units for transplant patients.

In 1980 I, along with Daryl, Fred Sexton, and Bob Sexton—whose wife, Sandy, had her transplant two days after me—purchased the Brentwood Motor Inn Properties, located a short distance from the clinic. Kidney patients could get rooms there at a reduced rate, allowing them to keep the focus on their immediate medical needs.

As important and helpful as this was, I still had even bigger dreams. I was determined to find a place that could be a home away from home for those on the transplant journey—a place where they could share their experiences and concentrate on getting better, and not be concerned about finances. Although I had no preconceived idea of what the home would look like, I knew I wanted something close to Mayo, with space for sleeping rooms, bathrooms, laundry, kitchen, and ample dining and family room quarters. The ideal structure would have been built in the days when boarding houses were prevalent, before the rise of motels and hotels.

The first person after my wife with whom I shared this vision was Mary Davie, who I'd met in 1974.

Mary immediately grasped the importance of the undertaking. In her job as a medical social worker in Mayo's kidney dialysis and transplant program she met with every patient, providing information and support with everything from medical questions to insurance paperwork guidance. She also had meetings with doctors and nurses where patient care was coordinated.

She understood that a lack of housing created an expensive burden that could jeopardize access to quality medical care. As a founding member of the Gift of Life board of directors and our first secretary, Mary's efforts were crucial in the early going.

I spent years looking for exactly the right property for our needs. Then one day in August 1984, I called her and in excited tones told her that I had a property to show her. I was coming right over to pick her up.

When Mary saw the 624 West Center Street property, she immediately felt its potential as a transplant house—a good thing, since I had already begun the process of buying it! Once the purchase agreement was signed, Mary assumed the role of Head of Household Operations.

There was no money for the first payment, or the utility bills. But lack of funds wasn't the only issue we were facing: The home itself needed a lot of work to bring it up to the standards we were looking for. Stucco was peeling and falling off. Chimney bricks were loose and crumbling. The walls were covered in as many as three layers of dirty wallpaper. The carpets were old and soiled, and laid one over the other. The front steps were crumbling.

While I worked to raise money from donors to meet capital expenses, Mary coordinated a large rummage sale that earned enough money to cover day-to-day expenses for a few months. This was the first of many fundraisers that helped defray the operational costs.

Volunteers worked tirelessly to make the house habitable. From July through December, a dedicated team went through the time-consuming, arduous tasks of stripping wallpaper, pulling up carpet, and hauling and cleaning furniture. A kidney transplant patient from an area college brought several friends to help strip wallpaper for a weekend. Another transplant patient who happened to be a plumber got the radiators in good working order. The local painter's union donated their time and materials, painting the entire interior of the home. The Rochester *Post-Bulletin* ran an article that brought in donations of furniture, linens, and more.

Slowly but surely the house was reaching its full potential.

Mary was also in charge of establishing guidelines for the transplant house and guests. The goal was to keep them comfortable and relieve their stress while doing everything possible to protect their health and facilitate their recovery. Mary researched policies and procedures from other hospitality houses. One of our primary models was the Ronald McDonald House network.

Because the Gift of Life Transplant House wasn't equipped to provide direct medical care, every guest would be required to have their own caregiver. Support for caregivers was also very important because they had so many responsibilities in the face of adversity.

Cleanliness was essential because so many of our guests were immunosuppressed and vulnerable to illness. Everyone had to clean the kitchen after every meal, and laundry facilities and cleaning supplies were provided to help guests and caregivers keep their bedrooms and bathrooms clean. The housekeeping staff took care of cleaning the common areas.

A key provision of the program was that no televisions were allowed in the bedrooms. This encouraged the guests to move around and interact with others. Televisions were available in common areas.

Finally the house was ready and the policies and procedures were in place. It was December 10ᵗʰ and I was anxious to take Mary for one final walk-through before the arrival of our first guest, Nancy from Mankato, Minnesota. When I called Mary, I was just as excited as the day I had called to tell her about the property four months before.

As she got into my car I said, "The house looks perfect. You're going to love it!" Then I added: "But first I need to pick up Jayne and Aaron at the hospital."

Mary was shocked. "Ed—I can't go with you to pick up your wife and your newborn from the hospital. That's a family thing!"

"Of course you can," I said. "Besides, I need someone to carry the flowers."

We went to the hospital and picked up Jayne and the baby. And Mary helped carry the congratulatory flowers to the car.

   *

In those early days, the check-in process was a bit involved. Transplant patients would come to pick up the keys at the motel we'd purchased next to Methodist Hospital. They'd check in, then walk to the Transplant House five blocks away. When they went home, they'd clean their room, come back to the motel, and check out. Those who could afford it would pay seven dollars per night. Suffice it to say, we were full in no time as word spread to other patients.

It wasn't long before the Gift of Life Transplant House was making a noticeable difference in the lives of guests. Doctors told Mary about the improvement in patients who stayed at the house.

On August 17, 1987, the $100,000 mortgage on the Gift of Life Transplant House was retired. The final $10,000 was paid by Mayo. The clinic had agreed to make that payment if the program was successful. This achievement represented the culmination of years of heartfelt work by thousands of caring, dedicated people.

But there was no time to rest. The program's success had led to increased demand. A new Executive Director would help us expand even more.

The original Gift of Life Transplant House and the original
board: Mary Davie, me, Dr. Sylvester Sterioff, and Greg Warner.
*Photo courtesy of the Rochester **Post-Bulletin**.*

Interlude: "Bumps in the road"

The Gift of Life Transplant House is a therapeutic place. The staff and volunteers go to great lengths to create a welcoming, family-like atmosphere that mirrors the optimism and hope by which I try to live my life.

This is where guests take the first tentative steps in their "new normal"—their post-transplant life—and get back into the world at large. For many, leaving the hospital after a transplant can be a trying experience. With its doctors and nurses, the hospital provides a sense of security. Most are discharged before they've fully recovered, with the majority of their convalescence taking place outside the hospital's walls, freeing space for those with more urgent medical needs. Being at the Gift of Life Transplant House is reassuring for guests who get encouragement and information from those at various stages throughout the transplant journey. This attitude is reflected in the pet names that guests have created for the house, including "the ranch," "the cabin," "the villa," and "vacation in the south" ("It's time to make our yearly trip to the ranch...").

Every year the Gift of Life Transplant House offers comfort and support to thousands of caregivers and guests. Not only are they the reason for the house's existence, each one of them is an important part of the house's success. Their stories are inspirational and demonstrate the power of the human spirit.

Of vital importance to guests at the Gift of Life Transplant House is the fact that they get to see former transplant patients who have returned for follow up appointments. Just as I learned early in my own transplant journey, seeing transplant recipients who have "made it" provides inspiration for those who are still in the early stages of the process.

Patients refer to the mishaps and complications that often arise post-transplant as "bumps in the road." They happen to everyone, but having the support of a group of people who understand exactly what you're going through is a crucial component of a successful transplant journey. Among those in the house are pre-transplant and post-transplant patients, as well as those returning for their yearly checkups. This mixture of people creates a built-in support group, aiding in recovery by giving especially meaningful information and creating a positive, hopeful environment that contributes to the healing process.

It's not just the patients who benefit. The caregivers are empowered with tools that enable them to help their loved ones and themselves stay strong. Caregivers face a lot of pressure throughout the process, and the Gift of Life creates a mood that helps bolster their strength, and lets them know that they're not alone.

Guests find an unexpected sense of community which manifests itself in surprising ways. There are bingo nights. The porches with their rocking chairs are favorite gathering spots. Each house has its own libraries and games; guests often crisscross back and forth across the campus. The communal kitchen is a place where guests spend time together sharing food and recipes, and having impromptu salsa tasting contests, ribs contests, and cooking presentations. There's also a free shuttle available to take guests to the Mayo Clinic and Mayo Clinic Hospitals, nearby grocery and department stores, but guests with cars often volunteer to drive others to and from the Gift of Life Transplant House.

*

One of the most serious health issues that transplant patients—especially stem cell transplant patients—face is immunosuppression. In order for the stem cells to take effect, a patient's immune system has to be suppressed to near zero. For this reason, cleanliness is vitally important wherever transplant patients stay. While a hotel might be clean, housekeeping doesn't take the same care that's taken at the transplant house. Those who stay in a hotel expend a lot of time and energy carefully cleaning their rooms and tables themselves. At the Gift of Life Transplant House, that's one less thing for them to worry about.

Life in the transplant house can be difficult before and after the procedure. Immunosuppression and loss of strength are only two of the physical challenges patients face. Many who have gone through the transplant process find it difficult to eat, feeling nauseated even at the thought of food.[3]

*

Jan Lewis's lung disease meant that she had to make the trip

---

[3] The favorite food for recent transplant patients is Kraft Mac & Cheese. It's generally the only thing they can keep down. And the fancy stuff, homemade macaroni and cheese with a variety of cheeses, is often too rich for them to handle.

from Oregon to Rochester about once a year for fifteen years. Gradually her condition worsened, and was complicated by other medical issues including connective tissue problems. It was nearly six weeks before she went on the transplant list, during which she spent time in expensive and impersonal hotels.

Among the paperwork she received from Mayo was a brochure with information on the Gift of Life Transplant House.

She returned from Oregon some time later for an interview and to take a tour of the house. At first, Jan was concerned because she's not always the most social person, and there are many communal areas throughout the campus. But the three houses are set up to accommodate everyone and all personality types; the campus is defined by its unpretentious, homey atmosphere. The rooms are comfortable and perfect for those times when you need to be alone but the communal areas are great for when you want company.

Jan needed to be within four hours of the hospital for her lung transplant. She and her husband Justin returned to their home in Oregon, but they felt a great deal of anxiety because the flight from Oregon to Minnesota is about three and a half hours—by private plane. For six months they waited in Oregon, and there was stress any time the phone rang. They always had their suitcases ready. If one of them had to run an errand or leave the house even for a few hours it was important to make detailed plans for what they'd do if they got the call from Mayo.

When a room became available in the autumn, Jan and Justin moved into the Gift of Life Transplant House. There they met people from all walks of life—rich and poor, farmers, mechanics, truck drivers, professors, musicians, writers, and more. Illness affects everyone.

Some of the medical tests that patients are forced to endure are embarrassing and difficult, but nobody at the Gift of Life Transplant House feels self-conscious. Everyone there knows and understands exactly what everyone else is going through. In your hometown it can be difficult having to spend a day with tubes in your nose or carrying a drainage bag; at the transplant house and Rochester in general it's an accepted part of the process.

Back in Oregon Jan went everywhere with an oxygen tank, and it was obvious that she was treated differently because of it. Others thought she must be unwell, and needed to be treated with kid gloves. At the transplant house she was treated as an equal.

Those who return from their transplant procedures are greeted by cheers and clapping from the staff and the guests. Jan watched seventeen people get lung transplants before her—each time she was excited and happy for them, knowing that those who received the gift of new lungs before her were either of a different blood type—or if they were the same blood type she knew she was moving a little further up the list.

Finally, after thirty-three months of waiting, Jan got the call that she would be receiving one of a pair of donor lungs that had just become available, and she needed to get to the hospital right away. She and Justin decided to leave the Gift of Life Transplant House without telling the other guests. Too often a call comes through that donor organs are available and an announcement is made, with other guests offering congratulations and sharing in the excitement and hope for what will be the beginning of a new and hopefully healthier life—only to have a problem arise that cancels the procedure, disappointing everyone at the house. (This is called a "dry run," preparing you for the actual event.)

On the night of Jan's transplant, a service organization provided a dinner for the guests. When neither Justin nor Jan could be found, the other guests deduced that Jan must have gotten the call. Jayne and I, who were in attendance that night, put together a plate of food for Justin and took it to the hospital.

*

Like me, Linda Vilmo suffered ongoing medical problems, the cause of which was misdiagnosed by doctors. After some prodding from me and Jayne, Linda and her husband Greg decided to make the trip to Rochester to visit the Mayo Clinic. Almost immediately the doctors there diagnosed her problem and told her that she needed a liver and kidney transplant.

I made accommodations for Greg to check into the Brentwood Inn and Suites, where he stayed for a month and a half while Linda was in the hospital. He didn't expect to be staying that long, and he quickly discovered that hotel life was lonely and isolating. When Linda left the hospital they were able to get a room in the Gift of Life Transplant House. Both had some trepidation about what the experience would be like. They weren't certain they'd be able to adjust to the more communal life at the house, but Greg found that it was like moving into a dorm. There was instant bonding with those who were going through a difficult time.

Although they made their home in Minneapolis, which is only

about ninety minutes from Rochester, doctors told the Vilmos that the closer they were the better their chance of getting a transplant. Every minute is crucial because organs can become available at any time, and as soon as they are available the clock is ticking on their viability.

However, as comforting and supportive as the transplant house is, waiting is still stressful. After seven months, homesickness finally overwhelmed the Vilmos. They decided they wanted to return home, but stayed an extra night to visit with friends who were coming to the transplant house from Iowa.

That night, they got the call.

Linda got what are euphemistically called "leftover parts." Because Linda was so small, she needed a transplant from a child. But the organs of children almost always go to other children. In the case of Linda's procedure, half of the donated liver went to a child, but the other half went to Linda. If the Vilmos hadn't been in Rochester that night, the chances are that Linda wouldn't have gotten her liver. Their story, like so many others, demonstrates the presence of God's hand in all our lives, as well as the miracles of modern medical research and technology—and the importance of the Gift of Life Transplant House for so many people.

Most people survive their procedure, but unfortunately there are some who don't. While the Gift of Life Transplant House is a hopeful place, there are periods of extreme sorrow. Everyone shares in the loss of a loved one. As Greg once told me, "At the house you learn to embrace life and accept death."

*

Kevin Dotson was diagnosed with a form of usual interstitial pneumonia (UIP) called Idiopathic Pulmonary Fibrosis. This is a debilitating and chronic condition that can be caused by anything from mold or toxins to chemicals. Essentially, Kevin's body was attacking itself, causing a build up of fibrotic material in his lungs.

His condition continued to worsen. His doctor in Fargo, North Dakota recommended he go to either Mayo or the University of Minnesota for further testing and treatment. He and his wife Dianna decided on Mayo.

They learned about the transplant house through the Mayo Clinic's pamphlet, and they were encouraged by a coordinator to check it out. They took the mandatory tour at the time when Kevin got his Mayo evaluation in November 2011. These evaluations went on for four to five days per week for three weeks. During that time Kevin and Dianna stayed in hotels, traveling back to their home in Park Rapids, Minnesota for the weekend.

Test followed test. Dianna had expected or hoped that the specialists at Mayo would tell them that Kevin needed a pill—that there was some kind of medicine that would alleviate his illness. They were both shocked when they were told that Kevin needed a double lung transplant.

Suddenly their lives had changed completely. Kevin's condition declined at a precipitous rate. Though he had an oxygen tank, working in their engine repair shop became more and more difficult. He lightened his own workload, limiting himself to a mostly supervisory role. As the days turned into weeks, Dianna hoped and prayed they would get the call from Mayo.

April 2012 was extremely bad. Kevin had no energy and each breath he took seemed like an ordeal.

Finally, on May 25, 2012, the call came through. They made the drive to Rochester, and Kevin got his new lungs. Both Kevin and Dianna felt they could breathe easier—literally and figuratively. Once they knew the date of Kevin's release, they put their names on the list for a room at the transplant house. Kevin would have to be near the clinic for at least ninety days following the procedure.

Dianna moved into the house a couple of nights before Kevin was discharged from Mayo. She felt a swirl of emotions— everything felt so unsettled, with a mixture of fear and relief.

Their second night in the house, after Dianna had made Kevin dinner, they were walking back to their room. Suddenly, Kevin felt light-headed and dizzy. Grabbing the hallway handrail he said, "I need to sit down—now."

Dianna helped him lower himself to the floor. Almost before she knew what was happening, the two of them were surrounded by caregivers. "How can we help?" they asked. "What can we do?"

Someone produced a cold washcloth and put it against Kevin's forehead. Two people helped to lift Kevin into a wheelchair.

Dianna, still reeling with anxiety and confusion asked, "What should we do?"

"Let's see how he does," someone said.

Two caregivers stayed by their side until Kevin's condition began to improve. It was their first indication that in the Gift of Life Transplant House, Dianna and Kevin weren't alone. They were surrounded by help—not just from the caring staff but the other caregivers and patients. Dianna felt a renewed sense of hope and comfort.

"We're here," she told herself. "We can do this…"

As it happened, Kevin's dizzy spell was caused by a problem with his medication. The next day, doctors adjusted his dosage and the issue was resolved.

After a few days, Dianna left to tend to their engine repair business, and their college-age daughter Emily took over caregiver duties. The following week, Kevin suffered another incident—once again, caregivers were there to help Emily look after her father.

Emily got everything from emotional support to cooking advice. The Dotsons all made lifelong friends that they continued to write, call, and text long after leaving the house.

For the initial follow-up visits, the Dotsons stayed overnight in a Rochester hotel. Because these were overnight trips, it made financial sense for them. But as the number of visits increased, they decided to stay at the house.

Following his transplant, Kevin's condition improved for a while. Unfortunately there were several harrowing complications, including perforated diverticulitis. Once when Kevin was in sepsis, he had to be flown to Mayo by helicopter.

The staff at the house always remembered them, and always checked in to see how they were doing. As soon as they knew they had to return to Mayo, Dianna would place a call or text to one of the staff so they could be put on the list for a room. Sometimes the call would occur in the middle of the night, right before an all-night drive across Minnesota.

As the return trips to the house became more and more frequent, it was clear to Dianna that she and Kevin couldn't have made it without the house. Not financially, and not emotionally. Hotels and apartments are too expensive and too isolating. Part of what makes the house successful is the support and encouragement that caregivers and patients provide to each other. Encouraging others promotes your own healing process. People need to tell their story—it's how they work through trauma.

Dianna came to this realization one day in the kitchen. A caregiver whose husband was dealing with a dangerous infection came into the room, crying. Dianna felt herself go tense. She was dealing with her own problems, she thought. She wasn't sure she actually had the strength to help someone else.

Dianna was relieved when another caregiver came in and put an arm around the crying woman. Then suddenly she was struck by the fact that *this is what we do here at the Gift of Life Transplant House.* Just as others had provided comfort and support to her, so too did she need to provide comfort and support to others. Not just for their sake, but for her own.

Once she'd finished doing dishes, Dianna took over, hugged the woman and listened to her while she talked about her difficulties. Diana provided her with the support she needed. Dianna found that living in the house opened and broadened her mind, and made her more accepting.

In October 2013, Kevin was diagnosed with Restrictive Allograft Syndrome (RAS), a debilitating condition that restricts lung capacity. It's exceedingly rare—Kevin's is the only post-lung transplant diagnosis in Mayo history. Thus far there has been a single study done on the condition, with a total of thirty-six participants.

Unfortunately, this degenerative condition meant that Kevin's journey would soon be coming to an end.

Before calling family members to deliver the difficult news, Kevin and Dianna shared it with the other transplant club members: The people at the house who understood what they were going through.

Mayo tried a lot of different treatment options. Photopheresis treatment seemed to provide some relief. Beginning in January 2014, Kevin received two treatments a week for six weeks. Dianna wasn't a very good driver, especially in winter weather, so staying at the house was an additional comfort.

Although they had hoped for a different outcome, it was hard for Dianna and Kevin to be sad, when they were surrounded by so much support. It was for this reason that they wanted to spend Kevin's remaining days at the house.

*

Will Oler was being treated for chest pains and weakness at the Virginia Hospital Center in Alexandria, with little success. For nine months doctors believed he was suffering from congestive heart failure, but his treatment wasn't alleviating his symptoms. In fact, his symptoms were getting progressively worse. Finally in January 2010 he got a referral to the Johns Hopkins Hospital in Baltimore, where doctors discovered that he was suffering with terminal amyloidosis. His doctor immediately made an appointment for him at the Mayo Clinic.

When he first got to Rochester, Will didn't know about the Gift of Life Transplant House and spent a week at the Marriott, at a cost of about one hundred dollars a day. During this time he was admitted to the Mayo Clinic for observation, and he was told about the house. His girlfriend, Robbye, was able to secure a room while Will went into the intensive care unit.

Will's entire body was beginning to fail.

Amyloidosis is a dangerous and rare disease that results in the over production of a protein called amyloid in the bones. This protein is carried through the blood throughout the body and its buildup can result in organ failure. By the time it was diagnosed in Will, his treatment options—already limited—had diminished considerably. He needed a heart transplant as soon as possible. Lack of proper blood flow had also caused his liver to deteriorate to the point that he also needed a liver transplant.

Will spent forty-seven days in the ICU before he got his transplant on April 25th. Amazingly, he was able to get both a heart and liver at the same time, from the same donor.

When he was ready to begin his stay at the house, Robbye put him in a wheelchair and brought him in through a side door. In room 136 of the new building, the manager was waiting to welcome him. It was Will's first indication of just what a special, caring place the transplant house really is.

For those first few days, Will wasn't able to venture very far from his room. The Mayo doctors had kept him in the hospital long enough that he'd recovered the strength to do simple tasks on his own, but even walking down the hall would leave him exhausted.

Slowly, his strength returned. He built enough stamina to walk around the house, then to the porch, then up and down the steps, and then he was able to walk down the street to Saint Marys. Walking to the bus stop to take the bus to the mall was a major achievement.

Will's feeling of growing independence was bolstered by the comforting knowledge that the Mayo Clinic was just down the street.

The transplant house keeps bicycles for the guests and caregivers and, after some prompting, Will's doctor granted him permission to ride a bike to the Hy-Vee grocery store. He was able to pedal there, but, unfortunately, his atrophied quad muscles made it impossible for him to pedal back. He ended up having to shuffle home.

Will ventured out to the communal areas, where he spent time meeting others who understood his medical issues. He got a great sense of comfort from the family-like atmosphere.

As an avid amateur chef, Will especially enjoyed being in the kitchen, which was fully stocked with every utensil and tool you could hope for, including barbecue gas grills. All he had to do was bring food. For the first week, Will was too weak to chop anything, let alone actually cook something. As his strength returned, he and other guests shared with each other, with people offering to help with washing dishes or vegetables. And once the cooking was finished he and the other guests had time to sit and eat and meet with people.

To this day, Will looks forward to cooking during his yearly follow-up trips.

*

The transplant journey is difficult to explain. Unless you've experienced it firsthand you can't really know what it's like. At the Gift of Life Transplant House, guests are able to share stories and build friendships around this shared, unique experience. The bonds last a lifetime, becoming a huge part of their ongoing social life. The effects ripple well beyond these relationships, touching every aspect of their lives.

People stay connected long after they've left the walls of the Gift of Life Transplant House. The community is worldwide, consisting of a fraternity of those who have experienced something that is unique, encompassing all the sorrows and joys that life has to offer.

Chapter Seven: A growing accomplishment

The eight bedrooms were always full, and not everyone who needed a place to stay could be accommodated. As Mayo expanded its transplant program to include liver and bone marrow transplants, the need for space only increased. It was clear we needed to expand. In the meantime, the entire Gift of Life board went searching for suitable housing to supplement the current facility. We found that Saint John's Convent wasn't occupied, so I looked into the possibility of renting it, until a new residence could be designed and built.

Consisting of twelve bedrooms, Saint John's would more than double our capacity. Mary called two people who served on the church council and they supported the idea of expanding the transplant house to the convent. We presented the proposal to the church council and after some negotiation an agreement was reached. The Gift of Life Transplant House now had a total of nineteen rooms available for patient use.

Even with the extra accommodations, it didn't take long to reach full capacity. Once again, the needs of transplant patients exceeded available rooms. This shortage inspired me and the rest of the board to continue our push for a new facility.

The partnership with the Franciscan convent didn't just expand guest space. One of the board members who was also a Franciscan told Mary about Sister Margeen Hoffman, who was then looking for a new project to which to devote herself.

Sister Margeen entered the Sisters of Saint Francis in 1954. She earned a master's degree in social planning and community organization—training and experience she put to good use during the Rochester flood of 1978, when she helped coordinate disaster response efforts among Rochester churches.

In 1979, she moved to Niagara, New York, and was a founder of the Ecumenical Task Force, a group consisting of Catholics, Jews, Baptists, and Methodists. The ETF was dedicated to protecting Western New York from the dangers posed by chemical contamination, and educating the public about the hazards of toxic waste dumping. Their members had experience with everything from civil rights work to health care.

From 1979 to 1988, she was the ETF's executive director, and guided the group's efforts against chemical polluters, including representing New York residents against companies accused of mismanaging hazardous waste. The ETF was instrumental in providing relief to residents of the Love Canal neighborhood in Niagara Falls. In the 1940s and '50s, a chemical company disposed of toxic chemicals in an area that would later become a housing development where hundreds of homes were built. In the late 1970s, those chemicals spread into peoples' basements and back yards. The ETF provided logistical support and assisted with relocation efforts, working with area residents as well as state and local government agencies.

This incident gained nationwide attention and became a turning point in the modern ecological movement. Sister Margeen was featured in several New York *Times* stories on the Love Canal disaster, and made appearances on *Good Morning America* and other TV and radio programs. In 1987 she edited a book called *Earthcare: Lessons From Love Canal, A Resource Guide and Response.*

By 1990, she was looking for a new challenge. Mary called her and asked if she'd be interested in returning to Rochester—this time as a consultant for the Gift of Life Transplant House. The idea intrigued her; moreover, she had family in the area. She agreed to give it a try for a few months.

On January 27, 1991 she was named the Gift of Life Transplant House's first Executive Director. She'd continue in the position for sixteen years.

God put me and Jayne together for a reason. God also put me and Sister Margeen together for a reason.

Sister Margeen took Mary's rules for the house and turned them into a solid model that truly made it a "home away from home." She was an integral part of our success, bringing with her so many intangible, visionary qualities.

While I was always uncomfortable in the spotlight, Margeen was happy to be the face and voice of the transplant house. An imposing figure with a strong voice, she had a take-charge attitude, courage, eloquence, and a powerful sense of advocacy. She complimented me and was able to carry my vision, devoting herself to the Gift of Life House full-time while I worked and dealt with my medical issues.

In recognition of her innumerable contributions to the house the city of Rochester honored her by declaring her birthday, April 25, 2002 "Sister Margeen Hoffman Day."

She made a name for herself not just for her compassionate support of the guests of the Gift of Life Transplant House, but also for her incredible fundraising ability. She was renowned for her "soft sell" techniques. As she would modestly put it, the transplant house was "an easy sell."

On one occasion, Sister Margeen was at a restaurant where she saw Queen Noor of Jordan. Queen Noor's husband, King Hussein, was at the Mayo Clinic to receive treatment for lymphatic cancer. Sister Margeen wrote the Queen a note, inviting her to the Gift of Life Transplant House for tea, and asked her server to pass the note to her. Although the Queen was unable to accept the invitation, she did send Sister Margeen a check for $10,000.

Later, on another visit to Rochester, King Hussein donated $250,000 to the transplant house. The Queen also took the time to visit with transplant patients.

A few months after becoming Executive Director, Sister Margeen arranged for her friend and fellow Sister, Jane Frances Gregoire, to join her in Rochester. Sister Jane Frances was one of the Stella Niagara Franciscans, and had taught in New Jersey, Ohio, and New York. After that she worked in housekeeping and maintenance, and was a stationary engineer performing plumbing work and boiler repair. She was also a certified asbestos remover. Sister Margeen knew that with her experience, Sister Jane Frances would make an invaluable member of the team. However, the board wasn't sure that they had the funds to hire her.

By September 1991, we were able to find the money to hire Sister Jane Frances part time, as the Gift of Life Transplant House's facilities manager. (She took a second job as executive housekeeper for the Assisi Heights convent.) At the Gift of Life Transplant House she managed the day-to-day operations of the kitchen and housekeeping, as well as tackling any heating or plumbing maintenance issues that arose. She was also in charge of lawn care, grounds keeping, and snow removal. With her pickup truck, tools, and riding mower, she was a familiar and welcome sight throughout the grounds.

Sisters Margeen and Jane Frances were like another set of grandparents, always showing an interest in my children and their activities. To the Sisters, Adrienne was always Princess Peapod. Edward Paul spent a lot of his transplant house volunteer time working with Sister Jane Frances doing yard work and raking leaves. They'd often visit our family for dinners or take trips up to our cabin and we, in turn, spent a lot of time with the Sisters at their office/home. They complimented one another perfectly—Sister Margeen was the more "refined" of the two, classy and strong. Sister Jane Frances was more of a jokester who loved to laugh and wasn't afraid to get her hands dirty with yard work or plumbing.

They made it their mission to keep the Gift of Life Transplant House moving forward, and were instrumental in integrating the house into the greater Rochester community. While I had laid a solid foundation, the Sisters really ran with it, spreading the word and making others passionate about it and its goals. As Mary Davie once said, "Srs. Margeen and Jane were the dynamic duo who raised money, looked after the needs of the patients and caregivers, and truly made the Gift of Life a home away from home."
*

In 1993, Saint John's Church notified the Gift of Life board that they would no longer be able to renew the lease on the convent. It was now urgently important that we find a way to replace those twelve rooms for our expanding mission. Actually what we really needed was to not just replace those rooms, but to *increase* the number of available rooms.

The first item on the agenda was to find a new facility. To that end, the board had been assembling property adjacent to the original transplant house located at 624 West Center Street. However, as God willed or planned it, the Mayo Clinic had placed the stately and impressive Judd House on the market.

Dr. E. Starr Judd was an original Mayo Clinic staff member, and in 1904 he became chief of the surgical staff. He was one of the top surgeons of his day, well known throughout the United States and abroad. He would later serve as president of both the Minnesota State Medical Association and the American Medical Association.

The Georgian colonial house was built for Dr. Judd and his wife, Helen Berkman Judd (who was the niece of Dr. Judd's surgical partners Drs. Charles and William Mayo), in 1911. There, Dr. and Mrs. Judd raised five children. In 1931, the Judds deeded the property to the Mayo Foundation for one dollar. The Mayo Women's Club began using it in 1938. In 1971, the Intensive Psychotherapy Center was moved to the home from the Methodist Hospital. By 1993 it housed a sleep study research facility.

Located at 705 Second Street Southwest, the Judd House was only five blocks from the Mayo Clinic. The board decided to acquire it, and traded all of the property they'd acquired adjacent to the original house.

Moving into this larger structure was like a dream come true. This was an exciting step up, not just into a larger and more comfortable space—it was also a psychological milestone for everyone involved. The original house represented a major achievement, but the expansion showed that what we'd started was actually *growing*. The Gift of Life Transplant House was taking on a life of its own.

However, for the Gift of Life's purposes, there were some problems with the Judd House. For one thing, it had only four bedrooms—and because one of the bedrooms had a bathroom across the hall, it wasn't usable as a patient room. After careful planning and consideration, it was decided to build a thirty-two-room addition. The total renovation cost came to $1.2 million, which the board didn't have.

Of course, such obstacles hadn't stopped us before. I set to work securing the funds. First I went to the bank, which agreed to grant the board a $900,000 mortgage, on condition that we raise $300,000 in cash and pledges.

Norm Gillette generously agreed to provide $150,000. $75,000 would be personally contributed, while the other $75,000 would come from his father's foundation, administered through the La Crosse Community Foundation.

La Crosse, Wisconsin was the location of the Kwik Trip gas and convenience store chain corporate headquarters. As it happened, I had performed several real estate acquisitions for that rapidly growing business. Furthermore, Kwik Trip's owner, Don Zietlow, knew the Gillettes. I asked Norm, "Would it be all right to mention your family's gifts to the foundation when I see Don?"

Norm replied, "Go ahead—especially if it gets the Gift of Life House money!"

When I made a trip to La Crosse to drop off some information with the La Crosse Community Foundation executive director, I stopped in for a meeting with Don.

Our conversation moved quickly, as I told Don my transplant story and explained the important services the Gift of Life Transplant House provided. I then told Don that the Judd House renovation plans required a great deal of money.

"Well, how much to do you want from me?" Don asked, smiling.

I couldn't help but return his smile. "Honestly, I'm not a

professional fundraiser," I said. "I didn't come with any planned request. Any amount would be greatly appreciated and put to good use."

Don sat back in his chair, considering. "Is $75,000 enough?"

I wasn't sure if I'd heard Don correctly. "That's—that would be amazing!" I said.

Michael Staenberg and Rob Glimcher, owners of a development company that I was working with, came through with another $25,000.

I then went to my friends Bob and Sandy Sexton, partners in our Rochester hotels. They agreed to give another $75,000. Bob and Sandy and I have a special connection that goes back to my first kidney transplant. I first met them and their young daughters, Bobbi Jo and Gina, while I was on dialysis in 1972. Sandy was in the same position I was and, in fact, she had her transplant just two days after mine. On April 26, 1973, I had the distinction of being the last transplant patient to go directly to intensive care afterward as a matter of routine. By April 28ᵗʰ Mayo had changed the policy, and Sandy was the first transplant patient not required to go directly to intensive care.

In the intervening years, our families became so close that when Jayne and I made our wills, we selected Bob and Sandy to raise our children if a tragedy were to befall us. We have so many wonderful memories of spending time at Bob and Sandy's home on the banks of the Mississippi, enjoying Sandy's wonderful cooking.

When they made their contribution to the transplant house they asked that three rooms be named for "The Three Amigos." On the second floor of the 705 House there are rooms named after Sandy, Chuck Parker, and myself, with plaques for each. The friendship and love we share is yet another example of God's blessings in our lives.

The mortgage was approved. God had guided me to another successful milestone.

Designers at the architectural firm Yaggy Colby Associates began working with the Gift of Life board. Also on the team was Cheryl Laven-Mayer of the Mayo Design and Construction department, a longstanding Gift of Life board member and past president.

In collaboration with Sisters Margeen and Jane Frances, the construction focused squarely on guest necessities. Because we didn't have excess funds, staff requirements were always of secondary consideration. This led to an awkward situation when the doors of the newly finished addition were opened in 1995. The combined executive director/house office consisted of a single 8' x 8' space near an elevator. The area was more suited as a copy room or a supply closet than a place to conduct meetings or to welcome incoming guests.

Upon completion of the Judd House addition, the Sisters moved into the original house located at 624 West Center Street. The lack of a proper office in the new facility meant their home would double as their office.

Obviously the expansion helped to meet guest needs. There were now a total of thirty-six bedrooms. Even so, it still wasn't enough to cover the demand. In 2000, a new expansion was begun, designed to add a west wing with thirteen additional bedrooms as well as common space we'd neglected to plan for in the previous expansion. The total cost of this expansion was $2 million, and the board had enough equity to borrow the full amount. It was dedicated in 2003 in Norm Gillette's name. A staunch supporter of the Gift of Life Transplant House from the beginning, Norm provided the $500,000 donation that retired the mortgage.

Despite the fact that we now had a total of forty-eight available bedrooms, as many as nine hundred families had to be turned away every year. Non-stop fundraising paid for the mortgage and maintenance on the house, but the board and I hoped to expand even more to meet some of the demand. Unfortunately, my dedication and determination would be tested once again, as I faced yet another daunting medical challenge.[4]

---

[4] Next door to the Judd House there stood a smaller, three-bedroom structure at 714 1ˢᵗ Street SW. This home was known as the Founder's House, in my honor. I had always resisted the board's offer to name the transplant house after me directly, and calling this structure the Founder's House was a good compromise. Renovating and updating the home to keep it up to our standards would have required a substantial financial outlay, so in August 2016 the building was torn down to add more parking space.

Sisters Jane Frances and Margeen

Norm Gillette and me at the dedication of his wing

My mother Helen

Drs. John Woods and Mikel Prieto and me

Chapter Eight: Gifts of love and life

For almost thirteen years following my marriage, I experienced remarkably few medical problems. Finally, in 1993, I had to have my left hip replaced.

My hip problems had lingered for decades. As part of my treatment, doctors advised me to remain as active as possible, so I went for frequent walks. In 1973, I started noticing pain in my left hip. This was the first indication that I was developing aseptic necrosis, a form of bone deterioration caused by a lack of blood supply. Hip problems are actually quite common for transplant patients—a lot of patients have both hips replaced soon after their procedure. It's a side effect attributed to prednisone, the anti-inflammatory drug commonly prescribed to transplant patients. Other side effects can include cardiovascular disease and skin cancer.

Due to a history of medical problems, my body doesn't have normal muscle capacity and my recuperative powers are greatly diminished in comparison with most people. Recovery following my hip replacement was slow, and in the process I had to deal with an infection that made things much more difficult for me. Walking was an excruciating ordeal. I tried to keep my spirits up and take inspiration from my growing family to help me work through the pain and get better. My life story is a litany of health struggles. I simply make allowances for these difficulties and continue moving forward with my life.

Staying healthy is all about maintaining balance. My early illnesses caused a great deal of damage to my body, so close and careful monitoring of my health status is a necessity. One seemingly minor problem can have deadly consequences if my doctors and I aren't careful. A positive attitude is a big component of my lifestyle, and Jayne, a tough Lutheran girl, is an important part of that.

In 1997, I spent a week in the intensive care unit following a triple bypass. Jayne was alarmed by my physical weakness—but even more distressing was the anxiety and fear that I was exhibiting. She knew that she had to be strong for me, to give me some of her strength to get past this difficult time. Although she didn't want them to see their father like this, she brought Edward Paul, Aaron, Nick, and Adrienne to visit me in the hospital.

"Edward, I need you," she told me. "We have four young children. You can't give up. This is why we have to get you out of here."

My recovery from the triple bypass was a long, arduous process. I found motivation not just from my family, but my work for the transplant house, my community volunteer efforts, and my work as a realtor.

Despite all of these health challenges, Jayne and I always made sure that the kids understood that they were loved and would be well provided for. I worked tirelessly to meet our financial needs, but unfortunately my health problems limited me physically. Jayne had to take care of a lot of the housework—including everything from cleaning and maintenance to lawn mowing. She was able to utilize her strong organizational skills to ensure that someone was always there to pick up the kids from sporting events or to take them to music lessons. There were also standing engagements such as regular Tuesday choir practices and piano days, as well as parties and crafting get-togethers.

Thankfully, our family was blessed with a support system that included friends like Sandy Silber, who would come over to help with reading bedtime stories, making meals, or comforting the kids when Jayne and I were dealing with medical issues.

Jayne kept things as "normal" as possible, acting as the family's rock. Everyone was able to draw strength from her, and she worked hard to strike a balance between keeping the children informed and protecting them from stressful information. Even so, my ongoing medical issues were always a part of their lives, and they were always at least dimly aware of my ongoing medical issues.

Nick felt "older" than his friends, because my health problems forced him to grow up quicker. He understood just how fragile life was in a way that most children don't have to face. Although his first memory of a serious medical issue was my triple bypass, my illnesses and hospitalizations—which averaged to about once a year—were just an aspect of life that he and his siblings dealt with. And then there were Jayne's reminders to me to "be sure and take your pills," which were a constant refrain.

I did my best to engage in normal activities with the kids. Although I had a good deal of difficulty running, the kids and I enjoyed playing baseball together. I brought the kids with me to check out the Judd House and the convent at Saint John's, where they ran around and played hide-and-seek.

The kids also helped me and my mother out at the Brentwood

Inn and Suites, which I owned. She would sit at the front desk and help check people in, then have the kids write room numbers on post-it notes which they would attach to the reservation cards. Another of their responsibilities was to use flashlights and rulers to look under the vending machines for loose coins.

After "going to work," I would take the kids to the coin shop, and then the baseball card shop. I felt it was important for the kids to have hobbies, and I would explain that "Coins are a good investment, but I want you to have fun, too. So coin collecting is a practical hobby, while baseball cards are for fun."

*

Jayne and I began to notice that I was running low on energy and my customary enthusiasm. I was also putting on weight.

Once again, I was to undergo a series of tests to determine the cause of my symptoms. Technology had changed drastically in the years since my first medical challenges, and my doctors and I had decades of knowledge and expertise to draw from. By the mid '90s, it was a fairly easy diagnosis to make: the kidney that my mother had donated was beginning to fail. Her kidney was obviously older than I was, and it's not uncommon for transplant patients who have received donor organs from a parent to need another transplant.

I was able to continue with my life mostly as before. There was no pain, although I did have to deal with occasional buildups of fluid. At first, I shared the news only with Jayne. We decided to wait as long as possible and do everything we could to maximize the kidney's lifespan before telling anyone else or making any concrete plans about how to proceed. Jayne, my nephrologist Dr. Tom Schwab, and I kept a close watch over the situation, carefully regulating my condition and performing regular checkups.

*

On June 9, 1999, I got the news that my father had died. I still had fond memories of spending time with my father before my horrifying medical problems began—of throwing a baseball together, learning to ride my first bike, and the amazing taskababs and Armenian pita that he loved to cook. As my real estate company grew, my father provided me with savvy business and investment advice, as well as tutelage and business loans. Jayne and I took the children to visit him once or twice a year, allowing them to maintain a strong connection.

My mother and father had a strained relationship. My mother

had a difficult time forgiving him for not coming with us to Rochester in the first place. My father had two jobs back in Michigan: he ran a boarding house for old age pensioners, and he continued to work at General Motors. He sent us money so that we wouldn't have to work in Rochester.

My parents each had their own ways of dealing with my illness—unfortunately, those coping mechanisms were incompatible. In many ways, my father was the opposite of my mother. While my mother freely expressed her emotions (you were never in any doubt as to where you stood with her), my father was a calm, steadying presence. He was a man of few words, but his love for his family was always clear. He was distinguished, gentle, and calm.

I understood that my father was supporting me and the family, and I felt no resentment toward him for not being there. My mother was much less forgiving. A particular source of friction arose when Mayo's doctors told her to summon the family when it looked like I might not survive one of the procedures I had before the transplant. For whatever reason, my father couldn't make the trip. My mother was hurt, angry, and frustrated.

My father also enjoyed traveling, while my mother would rather have stayed home. He traveled across Europe, had a condo in Florida, and lived in San Diego at the end of his life.

My sister Sharon flew out to California to identify the body and bring back his ashes, which were buried in an Armenian cemetery in Wisconsin, where his mother is also buried. My children and I all helped with the burial.

*

In 2004, Dr. Schwab got test results that suggested it was time for me to start looking for a donor kidney. Waiting much longer could mean that the kidney, which was now operating at between 10% and 20%, would fail completely, forcing me to go back on dialysis.

Advancements in transplant technology meant it was no longer necessary for donors to be of the same blood type. Jayne offered to be a donor, but as Dr. Schwab explained, the best possible outcome would be had with a donor who was a direct blood relation. This meant that our greatest chance of success would be to get a kidney from one of our children.

Dr. Schwab could tell from the look on my face that this was difficult information for me to process. As he explained, "Most

75

parents would rather go on the transplant list than put their own children at risk. But it's important to remember that the risk is actually quite small. And your children are old enough to make up their own minds about it, and their decision should be respected. Your health impacts your entire family. Besides, would you rather you and your son spend a few days in the hospital for one safe procedure, or would rather your children drive you to dialysis three days a week for who knows how long?"

Despite Dr. Schwab's explanation, the news led to what might have been the most stressful experience of my life. The decision to have another transplant was a difficult and emotional one. My mind was a swirl of thoughts.

A father is supposed to help his children—not the other way around.

I tried to picture sitting down with my children to ask one of them to endure a major operation on my behalf. I spent a lot of time alone, crying and praying to God.

How can I ask one of my children to give up a part of themselves to save my life?

Finally, after long, agonizing hours, I made my choice:

I can't.

I would go on the transplant list and wait for a donor organ to become available. I couldn't bear to see any of my children on the operating table.

Jayne was upset when I revealed my decision. "You need to start thinking about yourself for a change," she said. "You've dedicated your entire life to helping others through difficult times, yet now you won't ask for help from your own family. We need you in our lives. Don't deprive us of the opportunity to help you now."

Through tears, Jayne was able to help me accept the idea that my children should be given the opportunity to help me. But this was only the first difficult step. Now the two of us, together, had to decide exactly how we were going to share the news.

Most weekends Jayne and I took the kids to the cabin at our lake property. The drive usually took about seventy minutes; it was during one of these trips that we would deliver the news.

The whole family climbed into our Suburban and started off. With each passing mile, Jayne and I felt our anxiety growing. Finally we each took a deep breath, and Jayne turned toward the back seating area and said, "Daddy and I have something to say."

From her tone, the kids knew that they needed to brace

themselves. In fact, they'd seen clues that my health was declining in an unusual way. Nick, then a senior in high school, had watched as my energy declined. This was a slow process, and at first he didn't think anything was out of the ordinary. After all I was often tired—I'd just seemed a little more tired lately. Edward Paul, at college through the most difficult part of the rejection, had seen me come home early and leave late for work, and come home for lunch to take long naps that often lasted several hours. Aaron had noticed my weight gain and fluid retention.

Jayne did most of the talking: "The kidney that Grandma Helen gave your father is getting tired, and he's going to need another one," she said. Although I was generally very calm and laid back, I was always far more emotional than Jayne, and often I found it difficult to maintain my composure. This was certainly one such situation.

"We don't want to pressure you in any way. I'm getting tested myself to see if I'm a good match. If any of you want to get tested you can, but there's no pressure at all."

We were careful to emphasize the fact that if any of them had any reservations about being a donor then I would get a donor through other avenues. We also explained that the donor needed to be at least eighteen years of age to be considered. That meant that our oldest son, Edward Paul, who was then twenty, and Aaron, who was then nineteen, were both potential donors.

Our younger son, Nick, then spoke up, pointing out that he would be eighteen in only a few months.

Just as Jayne had married into my dream, our children had been born into it. They'd grown up with transplant recipients who stayed at our home and shared meals with us. They spent time at the transplant house with the guests, and counted them, as well as Sisters Margeen and Jane Frances, as part of their extended family. Our home was always open to transplant recipients who needed a place to stay when the house was full. All their lives they'd been very close to people who'd lived through the transplant process. They'd seen their grandmother live a normal, healthy post-transplant life. They looked forward to transplant house-related events like the yearly golf tournament, and they'd even played music for the residents—Jayne played piano, Aaron the violin, Nick the trumpet, Adrienne the viola, and Edward Paul the trombone. They had an intimate understanding of what transplant patients and donors went through. There had been innumerable bumps in the road, but they'd always made it through, thanks to the three things that they always knew they could rely on: Faith, family, and friends.

Both Jayne and I felt such gratitude to know that our children were more than willing—they were eager—to help me get through this.

In the end it was decided that Edward Paul and Aaron would both be tested as potential donors. If there was any hesitation on either's part, Dr. Schwab assured me that he wouldn't take the organ from them.

But neither felt any hesitation.

We spent the rest of the trip discussing the situation and making plans.

Within two weeks Aaron, Edward Paul, and Jayne were tested to match blood type and tissue type compatibility, and given antibody testing to ensure my body wouldn't reject the donated kidney.

Doctors found that Aaron was the closest match. Somehow, he had an inkling that it would be him, and he'd been mentally preparing himself for the news. An analytical person by nature, he thought a lot about why he was the best match. He felt that of all his siblings, his personality was the closest to mine. We also shared many physical characteristics.

When Jayne got the news, she wasn't surprised. She reminded Aaron that he'd always been strong. As a child when it was time to get shots he would eagerly jump on the table. He was fearless when it came to medical situations. It seemed to her to be just another part of God's plan for the family.

Aaron felt at peace with the situation. It seemed like fate that Aaron had one month during his four years of college that he could take off. That month is typically used for school travel for educational purposes—usually to another country. Edward Paul had already taken a month during his junior year and taking any more time off would be difficult for him.

About one month before the procedure we went to the hospital where Aaron submitted to a battery of tests including a CT scan to determine which kidney would be best, an iodine test, and a full physical. And, just as my mother had done prior to her donation, Aaron met with a psychologist to determine that his motives for donation were solely a desire to help me—that he wasn't feeling in any way pressured.

Now that this was decided, it was time to tell the rest of our family and friends—with one notable exception.

My mother continued to work with me, and to provide encouragement and support to transplant patients. She was proud of our shared accomplishments and was happy to be able to help at the Gift of Life Transplant House by answering phones, talking to patients, manning the front desk, and fundraising.

She'd worked as a secretary for much of her life, and joined Wendland and Robertson Realtors along with me in 1975 in that capacity. When Daryl Engelhardt and I started our own real estate business, she went with us.

Over the course of my mother's secretarial career, the real estate business saw massive changes, becoming more and more dependent on computers. She was far more comfortable using her trusty IBM Selectric typewriter, and had a difficult time understanding why the office needed to change.

With God's help, in 2002 I encouraged her to retire from her secretarial work so that she could devote herself to helping others on their transplant journey. As a caregiver and a donor, she'd experienced all the physical and emotional difficulties firsthand. She loved spending time with guests at the Gift of Life Transplant House—and they always appreciated having her as a resource.

She occasionally joked about "being fired," but she thrived at the transplant house, helping thousands of caregivers, donors, and recipients. After all, this had been a part of her life since my transplant, as I often brought patients to stay at our home, or to just share a home cooked meal that she'd prepared.

Her laughter was a welcome presence, letting you know where she was as she entertained the guests. She was invariably surrounded by patients and caregivers, sharing stories and providing a sympathetic ear. In a trying time, she showed love and kindness. I was grateful that she was able to spend so much of her time there.

She was also an invaluable part of our family's support system.

My mother lived just a few minutes away, and was always there for the kids for any reason—whether I had a medical issue, we were going on a vacation, or Jayne just needed a little extra help. The kids loved having sleepovers at her home, and each of these visits followed a familiar ritual. The night of the sleepover, my mother would take them to the store where they could get whatever food they wanted—including junk food. (Jayne and I were fairly strict about what the kids had at home.) Then they'd have dinner, after which they were allowed to stay up as late as they wanted watching TV. The next morning meant a trip to Toys R Us, where they could pick out any single toy they wanted—within reason, at least.

Another activity that my mother and the kids engaged in was the gathering of grape leaves from the grape vine that covered the retaining wall in her yard. She and the kids would take the leaves and carefully wash and dry them, then freeze them in plastic bags for later use in making stuffed grape leaves. My mother was an avid cook of Armenian food, and the kids would help her make dishes including cheese pies. She made these foods from memory, with recipes passed down through the generations.

I knew just how hard it was going to be for her to accept that her son needed another transplant. I had to keep it from her for as long as possible. Throughout my life, I had been careful to calibrate my contact with her, and I'd often kept quiet about my health issues. If I called her too often and missed a day because of my health, she would have gotten upset. Conversely, if I didn't call her enough she'd get suspicious, and would call hospitals to see if I'd been admitted anywhere.

So I had always maintained an erratic calling schedule that adhered to no set pattern. If I was in the hospital for an illness or a procedure and I needed to call her, I would tell everyone to stay quiet and close the door. When I called I would tell her that I was just relaxing at home, and there was nothing to worry about.

It was important for me to protect my mother from knowledge that was difficult for her to handle. Jayne, my sister Sharon, my aunt Janet, and I went so far as to tell the staff at Mayo, our friends, and our church family not to say anything to her. With God's help we were able to keep the secret.

The night before the transplant was to take place, our family was at the Gift of Life Transplant House. As we often did this time of year, we'd gathered to visit with guests, serve food, and spend time enjoying each other's company. We took a photo together beside the fireplace. Finally, the time came when I had to tell her. I sat with her, took her hand in mine, and delivered the painful news.

Predictably, my mother was deeply upset. So much of her life had been spent protecting me, helping me through one health problem after another. Knowing that I was facing another transplant procedure filled her with the pain and worry that I had tried to spare her for so long. Not only that, she was also disappointed that the kidney that she'd given me thirty years before was failing, and that her grandson was now being called upon to donate his.

Eventually, she would forgive us for keeping the secret. In the meantime, however, Sharon had to persuade her to not go to the hospital the next day. As upset as she was, her presence wouldn't be a comfort to me—it would only add to my stress.

The next day, December 28, 2004, I would begin to understand at least some of what my mother had dealt with all those years.

The Mayo transplant team allowed me and Aaron to lie side-by-side in the holding area, as we waited to be called into the operating room. It was a wonderful blessing to get to spend this emotional time together. I fought back tears as I prayed that Aaron would go through the operation without difficulty and have a quick, painless recovery. I was far more worried about my son than I was about myself. Aaron spent most of the time reassuring me. I still felt guilty about asking my son to make this sacrifice for me. But as Aaron explained it, he didn't see it as a sacrifice at all, and he was happy to be able to give me the gift of life.

It was at that moment that I realized just how painful it must have been for my mother—to see her son suffering all those years—and to feel so helpless.

I thought of all the tests, procedures, and treatments she'd watched me endure. I thought of her wheeling me down the hallways of hospitals when I'd been barely able to see, my back in excruciating pain. I thought of all those days spent going through dialysis. I thought of my mother's tender and brave smile through it all, and I shuddered at the strength she must have possessed.

Sometimes it's easier to suffer yourself, than to watch it happening to someone you love.

Even though I was visited by physician friends, my surgeons, and even the former head of transplants, Dr. Sterioff, there was still the chance that something could go wrong. But I had faith. God had guided me and my family this far. Somehow I knew that everything would come out fine.

My first kidney transplant was the 167th performed at Mayo. I was almost a guinea pig back then. By the time I had my second transplant, Mayo doctors had performed more than 4,000 kidney transplants and a total of more than 10,000 transplants of all types. A lot had changed in thirty years.

After the procedure Aaron began to wake. The nurse wheeling him out told him, "There's your dad. Would you like to see him?" Aaron replied, "Yes," groggily. Around him he heard excited voices saying, "Everything went great," "the kidney's working..."

When Adrienne visited Aaron just a few hours after the procedure, he smiled at her and said, "That was a piece of cake."

Jayne told him, "Dad's sitting up and awake."

"He must be feeling better than me," Aaron said. He still felt unsteady and sore. Generally, the recipient recovers more quickly than the donor.

Later that very day, with Jayne holding him up by his arm, Aaron was able to walk from his room on the fifth floor to my room on the tenth. He was startled by the way I looked—my attitude was so much more upbeat than before, and the color had returned to my skin. At that moment, Aaron realized just how far my health had declined. It had been so gradual—over a period of ten years—that he hadn't noticed before.

In two days he was able to leave the hospital. I remained for another night, and was released on New Year's Day, 2005.

Once again, I had received the most precious gift of all—the gift of life. But there were still more challenges ahead.

*

The week before Memorial Day 2005, I went in for a kidney biopsy at Methodist Hospital. This is standard practice following a transplant, and everything seemed to be going fine for me, given the circumstances. I felt healthy and upbeat; Jayne and I were both looking forward to Edward Paul's college graduation ceremony the following Sunday.

Then, as we were walking through the parking lot, I started to feel intense chest pains, shortness of breath, and nausea. As soon as we reached the car we drove straight to Saint Marys. There, doctors found that I had suffered a heart attack, and two grafts from my 1997 heart bypass were starting to close.

The medication needed to treat the closing grafts would thin my blood, and because of the kidney biopsy this meant that doctors couldn't prescribe treatment for the heart attack. They would have to let the process run its course and let the grafts close completely. Only if there was a massive heart attack would they risk treating the condition.

This was a recurring theme in my life: treatment of one health issue is complicated by previous health problems, or treating one problem creates others. My doctors and I had to always be careful to regulate every aspect of my treatment for every medical problem, to ensure that my recovery from one procedure didn't affect another aspect of my health.

Because we didn't want the kids to worry—especially Edward Paul—Jayne and I didn't reveal the heart attack until after graduation, which I was able to attend. As always, we worked hard to maintain a sense of normalcy in the face of grave danger.

Norm, me, and Jayne

Chuck Parker, me, and Sandy Sexton—The Three Amigos

My mother and me

Current Gift of Life House Director Ginger Holmes

Me and Mary Ann Leto in March 2016

Chapter Nine: The right thing for the right purpose

Throughout my life there were instances where God stepped in to provide an opportunity for even greater success. In 2007, Dr. Schwab (a longtime Gift of Life angel and board member) told one of his patients, Abdulla al Hashemi, about the need for more space at the Gift of Life Transplant House.

Abdulla owned a piece of property directly across the street from the Judd House. He'd purchased the property at a time when the real estate market was low, intending to build apartments there. However, when Dr. Schwab told him about our need for more space, he generously agreed to donate the property. While he'd never stayed at the house himself, Abdulla knew our story and he believed strongly in what we were doing. There was one condition for his donation: He didn't want the property to sit unused. It would need to be developed immediately.

This presented several logistical challenges. First and foremost, the board hadn't been actively planning for an expansion. No funds had been raised; all we had was the donated land.

The other board members and I immediately went to work.

Abdulla wanted to see plans in a few days. Jose Rivas and Chris Colby at Yaggy Colby Associates put together a basic exterior concept plan within twenty-four hours. Abdulla liked it, so the board moved forward.

At that time, the Gift of Life Transplant House had about $1 million on hand. The board decided that if an additional $1.25 million could be raised, they would authorize a $5 million mortgage. The total project cost, including all equipment and furnishings, came to $7.6 million.

Further complicating matters was the fact that my body was rejecting the kidney I'd received from Aaron. My symptoms manifested innocently enough, in the form of a simple but persistent cough. I didn't think much of it at first—I was too distracted by the work I was doing—but over time I began to develop other symptoms.

A series of tests showed that I had a virus, and the anti-rejection medicine I'd been taking was no longer working. I was close to full-blown rejection by the time my doctors began varying my medicine. They were able to stop the rejection but in the process my transplanted kidney had suffered moderate damage.

That summer, as part of my treatment, I had to carry a drainage bag connected to a nephrostomy catheter which was stitched into my kidney through my lower back. I carried the bag like a purse everywhere I went, including to meetings at the Marriott hotel where Abdulla had a room. Abdulla had received a kidney transplant himself, so he was sympathetic to my situation.

Sister Margeen was also facing debilitating health complications. A nun of the old order, a master delegator, and a pillar of strength to everyone she met, she was now living with leukemia, diabetes, and heart disease. She spent that 4th of July at a gathering at our home, enjoying her favorite root beer floats and spending time with the family and friends that she loved and who loved her.

On August 3, 2007, she passed away at the age of 71. The grief that I felt at her passing would have been devastating under any circumstances, but when coupled with my own precarious health situation the loss was especially emotional for me and everyone around me.

Despite my grief and the complications of the rejection, I was determined to raise the money necessary to start the expansion. I knew that I still had a great deal left to do, and as God led me, I continued on with my work. The first people I met with were Norm Gillette's children, his sister Norma Vinger and her husband, and their two sons. I explained the pressing need for expansion, and we discussed all the times in the past when Norm, who'd passed away in 2004, had stepped up to give generously to the house.

I didn't have a number in mind. "A one-hundred or two-hundred thousand-dollar donation would be greatly appreciated," I told them. "But what I really need is a major lead gift."

They called me later to let me know that God had opened their hearts, and they were prepared to give $1 million. I would have been happy with any amount, so I was overwhelmed by their generosity.

My uncle Edward and aunt Janet Mardigian had been donating $25,000 per year to the house. Janet is my mother's youngest sister, and is only seven years older than I am, which I feel contributed to our strong bond. Throughout all my medical problems she was a reliable source of strength and encouragement.

I told them about the current project and the amount the Gillettes and Vingers had given, and they came through with a donation of $250,000.

In all, a total of $1.5 million was raised. With this money in hand the mortgage was approved, and the construction began.

Because land was so hard to find in that location, the board decided that they'd have to build an underground parking garage on the al Hashemi property. This added $1 million to the project cost, but it would ensure we wouldn't have to use the entire site for parking, while leaving room to expand to the west in the future.

As the planning continued, the team was careful to incorporate all the lessons learned from the previous construction projects. This expansion wasn't just going to add space for more guests, it would seamlessly blend with the existing space while balancing the needs of the guests and the faculty—from the ground up.

The 2009 expansion added thirty-six bedrooms on three levels. The total eighty-seven bedrooms constitute the largest transplant house facility in the United States. My vision is now a stunning reality making a real difference in peoples' lives—its success has been greater than I could have imagined.

*

In 1995 my mother published a book titled *Gifts of Love and Life*, detailing our transplant journey. She held numerous book signings at the house, before which she would spend a day or two picking out her dress, her jewelry and getting her hair done. She had four phrases that buyers could choose from to personalize the autograph, charging $8 for each softcover copy. She'd spend three to four hours talking with the guests, and she loved the time she spent with them. She also appreciated being able to give the money to the Gift of Life Transplant House at the end of the day.

My mother had seen it all, and was always eager to help anyone in need. From offering advice to making a meal, she was a giving person and an integral part of the family. Her intense empathy meant she internalized the suffering of others. It wasn't just my illness that defined her. Having spent her formative years in mixed-ethnic working class neighborhoods in Detroit, seeing others struggling had a profound impact on her. She was always driven by an intense desire to help.

She loved being at the transplant house, and had a job there up until 2009. At the age of 84, my mother was just as strong willed as ever. Those who met her for the first time were astonished to learn how old she was—she neither looked nor acted her age. She took a lot of pride in her appearance, wearing high heels, makeup, and jewelry every time she left the house. She was very much a socialite, and almost everyone who met her described her as a "classy lady." She had a great sense of humor and loved to make people laugh. Not even heart disease and diabetes slowed her down.

Then one day at a grocery store she fell and broke her hip.

At first she appeared as strong and feisty as ever. For her first appointment at Mayo following the accident she had her hair done, and wore hose and a nice dress—she looked much the same as she ever did. She talked about recovering quickly so she could get back to the transplant house, where she loved to spend her time. But I could see that her condition was getting incrementally worse.

She did make it back to the transplant house, but it was always in a wheelchair or on her walker. I told her that as soon as she got her strength back and was ready to work she could go back to her previous duties. Sadly, she was in the hospital more often than not.

One day I called Sharon and told her that our mother's condition had deteriorated, and she should come for a visit as soon as she could. Sharon was shocked. "On the phone she sounds fine," she said.

"She still has the same upbeat attitude," I said. All her life she'd been a fighter—despite the odds—and she was still fighting. "But her body is giving out."

Sharon came to Rochester to see our mother for herself, and to provide love and support. She'd always been there for me in my health crises—now she would be there for her.

In late 2011 my mother went on dialysis. I struggled with my emotions, seeing her go through what I myself had had to deal with for years. I'm sure it would be difficult for anyone to see their mother in such a situation, but my firsthand experience with the procedure made it particularly poignant.

My mother passed away on December 17, 2012. Twice she'd given me the gift of life, and been a beacon for me and for everyone who ever met her. She had given me much of her strength. She'd shown me that I should never take "No" for an answer, and to always fight for myself and my family.

This was the woman who had played the piano while I sang songs, taken me and Sharon to Hudson's once a month to shop, wheeled me down numerous hospital hallways, moved with me to

Rochester to begin a new life, and dedicated herself to helping improve the lives of transplant patients...

I was overcome with grief to see my mother, my strongest advocate, leave this life. But I took solace in the knowledge that her suffering was over and that God had called her home.

*

Jayne and the kids and I have taken innumerable trips together through the years. I've always been deeply invested in history, in particular pre-Revolutionary War history, and many of our trips reflected that love. We traveled to historical places like Mackinac Island, Valley Forge, Gettysburg, Williamsburg, Philadelphia, and more. My oldest son, Edward Paul, shares my love of history, and has dedicated his life to imparting that love to others.

After graduating in 2005 from St. Olaf College with a BA in History—and earning a departmental distinction in the process—he went on to get his MA and PhD in Early American History at William & Mary. His dissertation examined how trade and economics affected relations between Spanish and American governments, with a focus on the Venezuelan independence movement of the early 1800s.

Clearly, Edward Paul has a love of learning and teaching, and he's pursued his dreams by teaching at William & Mary, Mary Baldwin, and the University of Mary Washington. Today he's back at St. Olaf as a Visiting Assistant Professor of History. He and his partner Lizzie Anderson had our second grandson, Nazarian (Ari) Glenn Pompeian, on February 3rd, 2016. Jayne and I are humbled by his intelligence and dedication. Every day he inspires in us the same sense of gratitude and awe that we felt when we first learned that Jayne was pregnant.

*

Aaron worked for five years in the Research Compliance and Grant Management division at Mayo. He was part of the team that ensured government regulatory compliance on research grants, preparing reports documenting that money was spent in accordance with government regulations. It was important work, but it left him unfulfilled.

My partners and I bought a restaurant called John Hardy's Bar-B-Q from the estate of founder John Hardy. A few years later, I sold my stake in the company to a partner who passed away in 2012. His family's attorney approached me and asked if I'd like to buy back into the company. I along with two new partners—one of whom owned several Perkins franchises and the other who owned a meat packing company—bought the business. Knowing that Aaron wasn't completely satisfied with his work at Mayo, I asked him if he'd be interested in working at the restaurant, at least one day a week. Aaron liked to cook and enjoyed his time at the pizza franchise we'd owned back when he was in high school, Nick-N-Willy's, so he agreed. He started as a dishwasher, working one day a week.

Mayo offered voluntary severance packages in 2013, and Aaron took one. He bought into John Hardy's as a partner, and now works there full time. Thanks to his hard work, determination, and business savvy, John Hardy's is a high quality success. Aaron married his wife, Helen, in May 2014 and had our first grandson, Henry Edward Pompeian on October 3rd, 2015. Jayne and I are thankful every day that our children and their families are in our lives.

*

After graduating from college, Nick considered going into medicine or law, even going so far as to apply to law schools. He worked for a year at a Marriott in Minneapolis trying to decide exactly what he wanted to do when I called him and asked if he'd like to move back to Rochester to help with my hotels and my real estate company, Realty Growth Inc.

Nick had always felt an entrepreneurial spirit, and he loved working with people. Having grown up with the Gift of Life Transplant House, he understood the hospitality business on a fundamental level. I'm humbled by the fact that he shadowed me for a while in college. (Even when he was three years old, Nick often wore a suit and tie, just like his father!)

The more Nick thought about it, the more it made sense to him. He moved back in July 2011 and started in housekeeping, to learn every aspect of my business. Then he worked with a hotel manager. Today he owns Realty Growth Inc., the commercial and investment real estate company he purchased from me and a partner in 2014. He helps manage the Brentwood Inn and Suites and Brentwood Inn on 2nd in Rochester, while he and his business partner manage the Fairfield Inn and Suites.

The Gift of Life board approached Nick about joining them around that time. It was another idea that made perfect sense to him. The board had always been an incredible group of people, many of whom had been with it from the start, who had seen our kids grow up. Nick felt blessed and grateful to have the opportunity to give back to those who had helped so many and meant so much to his family. They reflected my firm belief that you should always work to surround yourself with the best people.

In 2013, board members asked Nick if he would consider serving as the vice president, and he again accepted the invitation. Then in June 2015 he was named president of the board.

Many of Nick's duties include fundraising, but he also has to help make decisions that the staff can't make themselves for practical or regulatory reasons. Board members also volunteer at fundraising events. It's very much a working board, and its members live for the Gift of Life Transplant House.

Nick possesses a rare combination of compassion and business acumen, and Jayne and I couldn't be more proud of him and his accomplishments.

*

Adrienne has followed in the footsteps of Jayne, her aunt Sharon, and her maternal grandmother to become a nurse. Like them, she has a selfless determination to help others get through what are often the lowest, most dangerous trials of their lives. Her entire life has been preparation, giving her a unique insight into the needs of those who face serious medical issues.

She graduated from the Master of Science in Nursing program at the University of Massachusetts Medical School in Worcester in June 2016, and in October she'll begin her nursing career as a nurse practitioner at Mayo—the institution that helped inspire her love of nursing.

Her experiences have taught her to be smart about health, explore every treatment option, and never settle for inadequate care. Her future patients will be all the better for having her in their lives.

I see the reflections of Jayne, my mother, and Jayne's mother in her. We're so proud of her achievements and the dedication to others that has endured in her.

*

When I was a child getting blood transfusions and IV drugs at hospitals in Michigan, I contracted hepatitis C. This was before hospitals tested for it—they didn't even know what it was. (Hepatitis A and B were first identified in the early 1960s and

1970s, while Hepatitis C wasn't identified until the 1980s, and it wasn't until the early 1990s that screening for the virus began.) In 2015, I was put on a drug that cures the virus,[5] and the drugs used to manage it were found to cause osteoporosis. It's a problem that I continue to struggle with to this day, and which would create several challenges for me at the start of 2015.

Because of my history of medical issues, I work hard to stay in shape and keep my strength up. My regimen includes a lot of walking—sometimes as far as two miles a day. In January 2015 I fractured two toes without realizing it. In February I visited my doctor who told me that I had a stress fracture, but by that time it was already healing.

In August of that year, I fractured my right tibia while exercising. Thinking the pain that I was feeling was just muscle soreness, I continued to walk on it for nearly three weeks before telling my doctor.

At the end of that month, I was supposed to attend the Gift of Life's first "Gala of the Decades" event. However, I found that I had herpes in my throat, mouth, and tongue. This led to a dangerous situation requiring hospitalization for five days, during which I was getting anti-viral drugs through an IV. At this time, I had to be taken off a majority of my blood pressure medications because my blood pressure had dropped so low during the hospitalization. I will continue to be on anti-viral drugs for the rest of my life.

*

I was home from the hospital for approximately a week, when I started to feel chest pains. This necessitated another trip to the hospital, where I remained for four days of tests. When my results came back as negative it was decided it was safe for me to return home. About two weeks later, I began feeling sharp, stabbing pains in my abdomen, accompanied by intense feelings of nausea.

The next day I was taken to Mayo for a CT scan of my bowel. If the results showed damage, they would take me in for surgery. However, given my history, surgery would only be considered as a last resort. What they found was a bowel obstruction caused by the slipping of part of my bowel through one of my hernias. (Yet another result of my lifetime of illnesses and treatments is the

---

[5] At the end of 2015, in another example of God's miracles, I was deemed to be cured of Hepatitis C.

weakness of the fascia under my skin and my abdominal muscles, which has led to an abundance of hernias, which often appear like bumps in my abdomen.)

My transplant surgeon, Dr. Mikel Prieto, used his finger to push the bowel back through the hernia. It was a painful process, but it was over quickly and relatively conveniently. The hope was that this would fix my problem.

Unfortunately, two days later, the bowel slipped through the hernia again. Because Dr. Prieto lives next door, he was able to get to our home quickly to push the bowel back through a second time.

When it happened yet again, Dr. Prieto asked Jayne, "Have you got anything to put in this hole here?" He pointed to the spot on my abdomen where the bowel kept slipping through.

"You mean like a wine cork?"

He considered that. "Not quite. We need something a little wider..."

Jayne found a rubber wine bottle stopper, which they placed in the spot in question. They then wrapped a binding tightly around my abdomen, like a girdle. This held the stopper in place, pushing down on the hernia to prevent the bowel from slipping through. Obviously this was just a temporary measure.

Reluctantly, Dr. Prieto told me that surgery was going to be necessary. Given my delicate condition it was decided the surgery would be done laparoscopically. The earliest the procedure could be done was the following Tuesday, meaning that I would have to wear this makeshift hernia plug for five days.

In that time the spot began to feel tender, so Jayne placed gauze between the stopper and my skin.

There aren't many places in the world that would even consider such a procedure, given my medical problems. It was possible that I could suffer a stroke or even die. The original plan was to wait at least a month before attempting the surgery. However, for me, there was little choice. I'd gotten through serious medical complications before—I trusted that God would once again take care of me.

In fact, lying in the operating room, I was overcome by a feeling of calm and peace. The doctors were very concerned that I wouldn't make it out of surgery, but I had no fear whatsoever about what was about to happen. Whatever God's decision was about my fate, I was ready. As the doctors and nurses were moving around me, preparing for surgery and explaining the procedure, I couldn't help but smile.

I closed my eyes, but I could see a light shining.

Over the course of my life, I had felt this sense of calmness and peace only one other time—just before my 1997 triple bypass surgery.

That sense of tranquility stood in stark contrast to the threat I was facing. The doctor found and repaired multiple hernias—in fact, he stopped counting after twenty-one. He sewed a Gore-Tex mesh from one side of my abdomen to the other, creating a barrier between my bowels and the lining of my abdomen.

I had been warned that this procedure would be accompanied by a great deal of pain. Pain was something that I was well acquainted with, having experienced terrible pain the past. But it had always come in fits and starts. The pain that followed this surgery was different—not so much in its intensity, but in its constancy. The sensation was of burning and squeezing in my abdomen, and it was relentless. It became more bearable at bedtime, unless I moved my legs or had to turn in bed, at which point the pain flared again.

I was told that recovery would take about two months. During this time I was unable to exercise or commit to any physical activity. I grew progressively weaker. My hemoglobin levels dropped to 8.8 grams per deciliter of blood. Hemoglobin is the protein in red blood cells that carries oxygen to the body. For most men, anything under 13.5 grams per deciliter is considered low.

My body was not getting the oxygen it needed. In particular, my heart was starving for oxygen. One night I awoke with chest pains and reached for Jayne. "Something's wrong," I gasped. She helped me take my nitroglycerin pill, but I felt no change in my condition. "I need to go to the hospital," I told her.

A midnight trip to the emergency room revealed that my hemoglobin levels had dropped to an astonishing 6.7 grams per deciliter. As a result I was having yet another heart attack. I remained in the hospital for treatment of the heart attack and to raise my hemoglobin levels. It was a slow process, and my inability to move meant that my already weak muscles were atrophying even more.

I tried to focus on the future, and what I would do when I got better. However, when a person is that unwell, it's difficult to think about anything other than just getting better. Thoughts of my recovery consumed me.

At the Mayo Clinic's cardiovascular center they had tailored an exercise plan for my recovery. My atrophied muscles were only part of the problem—I was still contending with the effects of my fractured tibia and foot. The treadmill was dangerous for me, meaning that most of my exercise needed to be done on a recumbent bike, which I rode five to six days a week.

I found I could sit in a cushioned chair, but standing for any length of time was a real challenge because of my muscle weakness. It was difficult to muster the energy or even the will to simply stand up, so great was my pain and inability to focus.

Gradually, however, I began to realize that I was getting bored. This was a hopeful sign—I wasn't completely preoccupied with the idea of just getting better. Jayne and I went out one night to dinner. Then another night we went to a movie. Then I was able to attend a Gift of Life board meeting. Slowly, I was returning to my normal routine.

On my first Sunday back at church, I was reminded that the doctors—who feared I might not even survive my most recent surgery—don't know as much as God. There are times when I wonder why it is that I have been able to overcome so much when so many others can't and, conversely, why it is that I've had so many troubles to overcome. Yes, I've always trusted my doctors, but ultimately it's God that decides the course of my life. My faith in God and in God's plan for me has been a constant source of inspiration, giving me a sense of comfort in even the most difficult times. Perhaps it was this faith that I felt before my surgeries, when I closed my eyes and understood that God was with me, always.

Although my medical difficulties haven't stopped, I've continued to focus on the future, looking forward to another trip to Florida for the winter and even making tentative plans for a trip abroad in 2016.

*

Guests at the Gift of Life Transplant House are asked to pay a once-per-visit cleaning fee, along with $30 per night, if they can afford it. Even if every guest was able to cover the suggested nightly charge the income would be far less than the house's yearly budget, which is approximately $1.25 million per year.

The mortgage is roughly $360,000 per year, while the operations for the entire three-house campus (including salaries, facility charges, maintenance, and supplies) take up about

$700,000.

The financial requirements of the Gift of Life Transplant House mean that the other board members and I have to be in constant fund-raising mode. Many people think that the house is directly affiliated with Mayo, but that's not the case. From the start, Mayo offered the Gift of Life Transplant House moral support, but it wasn't until 2005 that Mayo began donating $25,000 per year to help defray operations costs at each of Rochester's three main non-profit houses: Gift of Life Transplant House, Hope Lodge, and the Ronald McDonald House. They also offer matching grants up to $100,000 for capital improvements or expansion. That covers only a portion of the yearly costs.

The board has to raise anywhere from $200,000 to $300,000 per year to cover the shortage between costs and income. Regular fundraising events include wine tastings, a 5K run/walk, a "Trails4Transplants" horseback charity ride, picnics, a new ongoing "Gala of the Decades" theme event, and the annual Golf Tournament which in 2015 celebrated its 31ˢᵗ year.

Once the mortgage is retired, the plan is to put that money toward an endowment for an expansion fund. Even today, the house is forced to turn away hundreds of guests a year for lack of space.

*

In addition to my work with the Gift of Life Transplant House, I've always been actively involved with the Rochester community. For many years I served on the board of Rochester's Choral Arts Ensemble, a group dedicated to enriching the community through choral performance. I've been touched to receive awards and recognition that include the Rotary Paul Harris Fellowship, JC Penney Golden Rule Award, KVAM Choral Advocacy, the Paschal-Murray Outstanding Philanthropist, Rochester Education Association Humanitarian, Rochester Symphony Aspiring Conductor, and the Rochester Mayor's Medal of Honor. My professional designations include Graduate, REALTOR Institute and Certified Commercial Investment Member.

I also served as president of my church, and regularly give presentations to spread the word about the importance of organ donation. I think it's vitally important to remind people that organ and tissue donations make possible the God-given ability to give the gift of life.

For many years I was an officer and board member of the

Healthcare Hospitality Network (formerly the National Association of Hospital Hospitality Houses). This national organization helps boards and individuals develop, improve, or maintain their non-profit homes that help and heal. They serve those who need housing while undergoing medical procedures at institutions throughout the United States, Canada, and Puerto Rico. I provided the HHN with fundraising expertise. There's always a need for fundraising, and I'm happy that my decades of experience and my passion have helped inspire fundraisers all over the world.

On January 4, 2014, the city of Rochester recognized our achievements by declaring 2014 the Year of the Gift of Life Transplant House.

*

Our efforts at the transplant house have inspired countless others to join in the fight to help transplant patients. Those who have stayed at the Gift of Life Transplant House are among its biggest donors of time and money. Schools, Mennonites, businesses, and service groups have also donated. This work has had a ripple effect, inspiring similar projects around the country.

In 1997, the Gift of Life board's founding secretary, Mary Davie, took a job in the Human Resources department at the Mayo Clinic in Scottsdale, Arizona. On her first day in Arizona she received a phone call from a member of a group that had been trying for several months to start a transplant house similar to the Gift of Life. They'd put in a call to Rochester, and Sister Margeen told them to just call Mary.

Mayo Arizona doctors had heard about the success of Gift of Life, so they asked volunteers and Mayo employees to start planning for an Arizona version. The group had been looking at motels as models. It was clear to Mary that they were unsure of how to even start, so she immediately took charge.

She learned of a large property in Scottsdale called the Brusally Ranch that a generous benefactor had donated to Mayo in 1994. The six acres had been part of a 160-acre Arabian horse ranch, and it had a large Spanish Colonial style house with six bedrooms and a separate guesthouse, each with its own private bathroom. Up until then, Mayo had been unsure as to how they would use the property, but when Mary and a co-worker, Dana Cummings, toured the site they found it would make a perfect transplant house.

Mary and the Mayo Arizona administration, the Facilities department, and the volunteer board of directors that Mary had helped establish negotiated a deal that allowed the board to lease the Brusally Ranch space for one year for a cost of $1.00, with an option to renew if the project was successful.

Mayo Arizona provided funds for cleanup, plumbing upgrades, carpet, paint, and more. Furniture, kitchen and bath items, bedding, paper products, and more would need to be secured, and volunteers recruited to get the property ready to receive guests.

For Mary, it had a very familiar feeling.

Her first volunteer was her husband, Tom. Like Mary, he had extensive experience with the original Gift of Life Transplant House, as he was one of the original 624 West Center Street volunteers. Tom had retired from his position in the Rochester public school system when Mary accepted a full-time post in Arizona.

Tom wanted something more. He found retirement to be less than fulfilling, so he offered to act as an unpaid manager for the two to three months it would take to setup the house and take care of the facility logistics. Sister Margeen was an important resource once again, and Tom established operational procedures modeled after those of the Gift of Life Transplant House. There was even some talk of naming it the Gift of Life Transplant House – Arizona, but there were concerns over liability issues, so that plan was scrapped.

Opening on July 1, 1999, the impact of the Arizona Transplant House was apparent from the start. Its seven rooms were almost always filled to capacity. The original one-year lease was extended for two more five-year terms. Tom's volunteer position soon became full-time and Tom, who'd started stripping wallpaper and hauling furniture in Rochester back in 1984, was named Executive Director of the Arizona Transplant House in 2001.

*

Soon after the Arizona Transplant House opened its doors in 1999, a small group in Jacksonville Florida contacted them. They were planning on opening a transplant house on the Mayo Florida campus and were looking for guidance and information.

In the early 1990s, St. Andrews Lighthouse ran a six-bedroom hospitality house near the beach. After seeing the success of the Gift of Life and the Arizona Transplant House, Mayo wanted to have a similar facility on their Jacksonville campus. Knowing that Mayo patients often stayed at the St. Andrews Lighthouse building, Mayo asked them if they would be interested in partnering in the operation of Mayo's new facility.

Jorge Bacardi, a member of the Bacardi family—distributors of rum—spent many years of his life dealing with serious medical issues. Like me, Jorge's condition was misdiagnosed by his doctors. What they thought was cystic fibrosis was actually a disease called ciliary dyskinesia. A double lung transplant would be necessary to save his life.

Jorge had his transplant at Mayo Clinic Jacksonville. He and his family wanted to both commemorate his lung donor and give back to the institution whose doctors and researchers had saved his life. At the time of the transplant Jorge didn't know the name of his donor, so he dubbed him Gabriel, after the archangel. Jorge and his wife Leslie made a large donation to fund the new hospitality house that was then under construction and would house transplant and cancer patients.

In honor of Jorge's lung donor, who was later identified as a 19-year old college student called Christopher Mark Gregory, the house was named Gabriel House of Care.

The Jacksonville team, including Dr. Caesar Keller, the lung transplant chair, reached out to the Gift of Life board, and received valuable information, guidance, and insight. Before construction began members of the Gabriel's House board visited Rochester to see the Gift of Life Transplant House firsthand.

In 2011, the thirty-room Gabriel House of Care first opened its doors.

Among the facility's volunteers was a familiar face from the Gift of Life Transplant House: Sister Jane Frances Gregoire. She'd taken over as the Gift of Life's executive director after Sister Margeen's death. In recognition of all she'd done for the Gift of Life Transplant House, the Mayor of Rochester honored her by declaring May 17, 2011 Sister Jane Frances Gregoire Day. She retired as executive director later that year and moved to Jacksonville where she assisted in setting up the center, volunteering with the facilities and laundry. She remained there until her death on October 18, 2013.

I'm humbled to know that our efforts in Rochester were sending ripples across the world, and serving as a model for others who wanted to provide comfort to those facing life threatening medical problems and their loved ones.

*

Before the transplant house expanded, our family had friends over to stay the night or sometimes just for dinner when they were in town for their yearly checkup. The kids spent time with the adults, and often tried hard to be entertaining.

These visits showed the deep connection that was established between transplant recipients. The procedure is an intense experience, and those who have been through it share a special, irrevocable bond that transcends any superficial differences.

This connection animates the transplant house. The community building it represents is part of an ongoing network of support, understanding, and grief. The house is as much a product of the work of me, Sister Margeen, the staff, and its volunteers as the guests and caregivers themselves.

The idea behind the transplant house is a powerful one. I had built an informal network before, but my drive to found the house served as the foundation of a formal support network of people with a deep and abiding commitment to healing. Everyone is there for encouragement, but there are layers to the participation. The space is designed to promote interaction, which is one of the most important tools of healing available to patients, but there are also places for those who need time for themselves.

I had seen the emotional, psychological, physical, and financial toll that my illness had taken on my family. I'd seen the same toll exacted in other families. I had the wherewithal and drive to make it happen, and I also found the people I needed to help bring my vision to life. These are committed, devoted people who give their labor, time, and money in service of a network dedicated to fighting illness which is blind to class, religion, race, or socioeconomic background.

*

Through the years, I've been privileged to meet thousands of people who have taken advantage of the Gift of Life Transplant House's services. In 2014, I was one of five recipients of *RealtorMag*'s Good Neighbor Award. I consider it to be a collective award for the countless volunteers, board members, caregivers, and patients who have made the house a success. As they put it on the cover of their November/December issue, the Gift of Life Transplant House is "a haven built for healing." Our efforts have helped to ease the transplant journey for tens of thousands of people. In addition to the $10,000 prize, Internet voting added an extra $1,000 for a total of $11,000 for the Gift of Life Transplant House. *RealtorMag* also paid for a professional video for Gift of Life's use, and paid for Jayne and I to attend the 2014 national convention held in New Orleans to honor all the Good Neighbor Award recipients.

Finally, after many years of asking, I felt the time was right to accept the board's offer to honor me and Jayne by officially renaming the 705 house for us, in recognition of our efforts to build the Gift of Life Transplant House into the largest such facility in America. Today the structure is officially known as the Edward and Jayne Pompeian Home at the Gift of Life Transplant House.

Mary Davie once said, "If you're doing the right thing for the right purpose, it will all work out." Every day, I do my best to demonstrate the importance of doing the right thing for the right purpose. Throughout all of my illnesses and medical procedures— which have included two kidney transplants, open heart surgery, and two hip replacements, as well as extended dialysis treatments and numerous infections and immunosuppression problems—I've always tried to remain focused on my blessings, and accept each challenge as it arises. My determination to overcome every obstacle allows me to look forward to a bright and happy future without dwelling on past problems. My wife Jayne and I have unflagging optimism in the face of incredible difficulty. Having something to live for, building a strong support system, staying hopeful, and trusting God are all vital components of our philosophy. Despite all our challenges, we never give up, and look at each day as a gift—and always trust that tomorrow will be better. My children say I'm a "walking miracle." They say that not because I've overcome so many medical problems, but because of what I've accomplished through faith, family, and friends.

I am just one of the tens of thousands of people who have been blessed to have a successful transplant journey. While the types of transplants and the details may differ, we all share the same anxiety and hope. The ups and downs of the transplant and the side effects are all part of what joins us in the transplant community. The path we all must travel is full of many obstacles that with the help of God, medical personnel, family, and friends we can overcome. The transplant journey has given me the opportunity to meet and help others and brought me many blessings, including my wife, family, and a successful career. The journey has been worth the risk and effort.

The Mayo Clinic has been an integral part of my success and has allowed me the opportunity to live a full and rewarding life. There are no words that I could ever say that could express the depth of my gratitude to Mayo Clinic and all of the staff who helped give me the gift of life.

Where the Gift of Life Transplant House goes now and in the future I do not know. I am confident that with the help of God, the generosity of our donors, the outstanding board of directors, and great staff, the Gift of Life Transplant House will be able to continue and grow its mission until such time that transplantation may not be needed.

My family and I have been truly blessed by God and we are so thankful for having had the opportunity to have met and helped so many people during this fifty-year journey of mine.

My family at the dedication of the 705 House,
July 2016

Me and Jayne standing with the plaque commemorating the renaming of the house

Acknowledgements

My doctors like to say that the transplant journey is a marathon, not a sprint. In my case, the marathon began long before my actual transplant procedure—on that fateful day at Hudson's department store. With the vital support of my family, friends, doctors, and innumerable volunteers, I've been able to maintain my own health and continue moving forward. I'm grateful to everyone I've met on this journey.

Sam and Mary Ann Leto were responsible for telling my family about the Mayo Clinic in the first place and encouraging us to make that first trip in 1964. Thanks to them I found the doctors who would save my life and I found the city I still call home.

My God has orchestrated and planned my blessed existence. He allowed me to live a full life, to have a successful real estate career, family, and friends. I also want to thank Him for using me to start the Gift of Life Transplant House.

My mother, Helen, gave me her strength, tenacity, love, and caring when I needed and relied on her for everything. She was constantly by my side, encouraging me to continue fighting and keeping me alive.

My aunt Janet and sister Sharon were constant sources of love, support, and caring. They were always there when I needed them.

My father, Edward, provided financial support and, by learning how to dialyze me at home for three years prior to the transplant, provided much needed medical support.

Without my wife, Jayne, I could not have made it this far. She is my soul mate and my strength, giving me love, support, and constant encouragement.

Our children, Edward Paul, Aaron, Nick, and Adrienne have always been there for me during difficult times and have blessed my life in so many ways. They have truly made my life worth living. And once again I want to thank Aaron, for his unselfish act of love donating a kidney to me in 2004.

The Mayo Clinic has kept me healthy and allowed me to live my life to fullest. Mayo gave me the chance to live a normal life by allowing me to have a transplant during those early pioneer days of transplantation.

So many doctors have had a profound impact on my life: Dr. John Woods, who performed my first transplant in 1973, and Dr. Mikel Prieto, who performed my second transplant in 2004. Early

Mayo doctors in dialysis and transplantation, Dr. Ed Burke, Dr. Richard Wagoner, Dr. William Johnson, Dr. Carl Anderson, Dr. John Mitchel, Dr. Stephen Kurtz, Dr. Peter Fronhert, Dr. Jorge Velosa, Dr. Thomas Schwab, Dr. Timothy Larson and many others who have cared for me in all of the Mayo specialty areas. Dr. Franklin Sim, Orthopedics, Dr. Hartzel Schaff, Cardiology surgeon, and Dr. Brooks Edwards, my current Cardiologist, along with many others, as well as all of the allied staff at Mayo who have taken such good care of me. From the techs to the nurses to the radiologists to the entire medical team at Mayo—I don't have the words to express my gratitude and respect.

Special recognition goes to my doctor and friend, Dr. Tom Schwab. He has been my nephrologist since Dr. Carl Anderson retired, some fifteen or twenty years ago. He not only has been my doctor, but has dedicated his life to transplant patients and the Gift of Life Transplant House. If either I or the transplant house needed anything he would be there, no questions asked. He has pulled my wife and I through some of the most difficult times of our lives as I went through the myriad of illnesses I have experienced over the years. This is one great, loving and kind human being; a doctor who places the patient above all else and who goes that extra mile. He has spent nights in the emergency room with Jayne and I, when he could have been at home. The concern and compassion he has for all of his patients is exemplary. He is an amazing doctor and human being and I am thankful everyday that he is part of my life.

When Sister Jane Frances retired for health reasons, the transplant house was left without a permanent director for the first time since 1991. Ginger Holmes had been a valued volunteer who was asked to consider becoming the new permanent Executive Director. She accepted the appointment in September 2012. She is skilled at her job and has a love for the mission, as well as a deep compassion for our guests. She has proven to be a wonderful addition to the Gift of Life family and has been another of God's blessings.

I'd also like to recognize all of our present staff, dedicated and hard-working individuals who have answered the calling of our mission.

To all the countless other board members, staff, and volunteers over the past thirty-two years of the Gift of Life Transplant House: You truly are my heroes, and are to be applauded for your dedication and hard work. Thanks to your efforts, the transplant house is a place to be proud of.

Thank you so much to the first board of directors: Mary Davie, Greg Warner, and Dr. Sylvester Sterioff, who helped make my dream come true.

To all of the donors who have contributed their treasures for the benefit of transplant patients past, present and future: Thank you so much for your generosity and spirit. Those who made the house a reality with their major gifts: Norm Gillette and his children, Bob and Sandra Sexton, Don and Lavonne Zietlow, Norma and Don Vinger and family, Edward and Janet Mardigian, King Hussein and Queen Noor, Ann and Henry Zarrow and the Ann and Henry Zarrow Foundation, Mr. Abdullah al Hashemi, and many, many others.

The Ann and Henry Zarrow Foundation has recently pledged adequate funds for the transplant house to pay off its current mortgage and to start an endowment. What a wonderful gift from the Zarrow family in honoring their parents and continuing their parents charitable giving.

Lastly, I want to thank all of the transplant patients who have enriched my and my family's life. Norm Gillette, Bob and Sandy Sexton, Chuck and Brenda Parker, John and Kathy Kling, Luis and Angela Uribe, Mark Torgimson, and hundreds more transplant brothers and sisters—you have made my life complete. I am ever so thankful to have had the opportunity to meet these amazing and wonderful human beings. I also want to thank those that have provided testimonials for my story.

I want to especially thank Justin and Jan Lewis for their dear friendship and for encouraging me to finally finish writing my story, and their countless hours editing my manuscript.

Thanks to Ed Gorman for introducing me to Ricky Sprague and for Ricky's assistance in writing my story.

I apologize for any names I may have inadvertently forgotten as over the course of these past forty-four years I have met thousands of people who have been an important part of my life's journey. Know that you are always in my heart, with gratitude for the part you've played in my life and story.

My family 2016

My nephew Paul and his wife and daughter

Testimonials

"My husband John's kidneys failed in 1972, the year after he took his first job as a professor at a small college in Minnesota. Fortunately, we lived just 50 miles from the Mayo Clinic. After about a year and a half on dialysis, he had a transplant. Those were in the early days of transplants before much was known about the psychological wellbeing of patients and their caregivers. Things big and small often would go wrong, and it could be very stressful.

John had four rejection experiences after the transplant. During the worst of them, he was hospitalized and put on a very powerful antirejection drug. I was allowed to take John out of the hospital for occasional dinners in those days. One evening shortly after John was given the drug, I arrived to take him to a local fast food place. In the car, he obsessed about how my ten dollars would not be enough to buy two hamburgers. All through dinner he did not seem like himself and was aware of feeling different.

Since I was anxious about the meaning of John's strange responses and no one at the hospital had given me any information about what to expect, I turned to Ed Pompeian. Ed had a transplant the year before, and he was often a source of information and encouragement for the rest of us. He had spent time with John and had heard some even stranger thoughts from him than I had. Ed was the one who informed me of the powerful side effects of this drug and that some people who had taken it had hallucinations so severe that they were sent to psychiatric units. However, he also was the calming influence who told me that in most transplant patients he had known, it did not get that bad. During the whole time John was in the hospital, Ed checked in on him regularly and offered cheerful support. As it turned out, Ed was right and John got through the experience with his kidney and psyche intact.

Over the years, Ed has often been that resource and friend. He has a very positive outlook, which has been a good balance to John's more anxious perspective on life. Whenever the normal ups and downs of having a transplant have occurred, they have been able to discuss them and how they are coping. Even after we moved several states away, Ed and his wife Jayne have continued to share their home, their family, and their time when we come to town. Although the Mayo Clinic has grown tremendously in size over the years, the experience of going to Rochester has not felt as foreign as it could be because for us, Ed and Jayne have come to represent the best of our Rochester experience."

-Kate Kling

"Words simply can't express how grateful we are for you and Jayne and what a profound impact you have had. You have touched so many lives and lifted up so many who were in need. You deserve immense credit for what you have created and the legacy that will live on after all of us are gone.

Keep up the good work, you make us proud every day."
-Brooks S. Edwards, M.D.

"In June, 2007, I had a heart transplant at the Mayo Clinic in Rochester. Prior to the surgery, I was told I would have to stay in Rochester for at least 3 months following the transplant for recovery and rehab. I looked all over at apartments, motels, B&B's but nothing compares to The Gift of Life Transplant House. Not only did I recover better, but I made long lasting friends."
-Judie McConville

"A natural place of support and healing.

A special place where people of all walks of life become a support system.

A unique place that impacted our family financially and emotionally.

A place of beauty, cleanliness, and camaraderie.

A place with a staff and dedicated group of volunteers who have a giving spirit.

A place that has touched all aspects of our lives and continues to do so even today here in Oregon.

A place where we met terrific people from around the U.S. and the world.

A place where we met people who have become a part of our "family". People we think about and stay in touch with on a daily basis.

A place where caregivers and patients all touch each others lives in very special ways.

A place that allows us to both give and receive.

A place where you develop community strength by just being there.

The GOL is:

The 'the game changer.'

The 'right' place.

'Our home away from home.'"
-Justin and Jan Lewis

"I think most of us coming to GOL for the first time are a bit scared.

What will it be like staying in a big house, sharing spaces with a group of strangers, half of them recovering, but many still suffering from their illness? How will I fit in? Well, it didn't take long to become part of the big extended family living there.

Almost from the first day, we were taken in by a posse of new friends headed by Jim and Curt. The rocking-chair-porch became the heart of 'our' big old house. Everything was discussed there; life stories, fears and dreams, diagnosis, pee and poop, too much laughter, and of course food and the weather. Soon our circle included a group of nine couples! All except one room served by the west kitchen of the 705 House. We let Cindy and Judd join us from the other side of the house because Cindy liked to do puzzles, and she had a wicked sense of humor — poor Judd! We shared meals, caregiving/patient stories, and helped each other each day with the unexpected dramas. And we always filled up those rocking chairs.

There developed an unexplained closeness with this large group of new friends. We somehow bonded from our shared beginnings, even though we couldn't have been any different: teachers, banker, farmer, landscaper, nurses, executives, retail worker, day care provider. Rich and poor, and some in between, it didn't make any difference. We were one; we were those from 'the old house.' A fraternity of sorts, it was a bit like college again, living back in the dorm, learning to live and prosper with people of such different backgrounds.

And there was always the food. Talk about the 'freshman 15' – that quickly changed to the 'caregiver 12!' So many treats! But Curt brought us the first fresh asparagus from the farmers market, Ricky the first strawberries. Dennis was always doing something amazing on the gas grill; racks of ribs, whole chickens, fish. Carol taught us how to bake bread and cinnamon rolls. Dianne made granola. A bunch of us walked the GOL 5K. Darrel and I came in proudly last! And always we'd sit in those rockers, waiting to hear if someone had harvested enough stem cells, how their blood work came back, what their meld score was, watching the weather and the world roll by. And always laughing within each other's company.

And then came the day that some of the group were well enough to go home. Those were bittersweet happy days because we were all so happy for that accomplishment, but our new extended family was beginning to separate and head back to their 'real' home and life. But some of us had to stay, waiting for 'The Call', or for the transplant to take control.

And then we began to lose the first of our friends to the angels above. Three of our friends didn't make it. A man named Burton was sitting in the rockers one day, back for a yearly check-up, and he told me, 'You'll make friends for life here, but not all of them will make it.' Those were devastating times, watching a friend die for the first time, after struggling so hard to beat down that demon illness. Totally humbling knowing how vulnerable each of us are. (We ended up losing more than a dozen of our new friends, but oh so many more made it!)

Still the house enclosed us within its arms, with a much-needed sense of security. It's the history within its walls. There were so many spaces to be alone if one wanted, and always a shoulder to lean on. And out in the front yard, the two twin oaks stand sentinel in front of 'our' house. How much joy, happiness, and sorrow have they shielded?

Then our original group was all gone from the house, and I wondered: what now? But slowly another circle of friends formed, new bonds were made, and broken as they left, more puzzles done, more cookies baked and eaten. Even a leg of lamb was roasted.

We formed three different circles of friends at GOL. Each distinctly different, but also the same. They were our new family, our new normal, our lifelines, where nothing has to be explained. We would not have made it through this journey without their comfort and joy. Especially the love of Carol & Charles, Dianna, Kevin and Emily, who have ridden the road the longest with us. But what great new friends we have now in this late part of our new life!!! At a certain part of the day the sun shines through the crooks of those gnarly trees, the rays shining as the face of God, reminding us there is always hope."

-Greg Vilmo

Our Mayo Experience

Line up here—state your name.
    Is your birth date still the same?
Mayo number? We'll scan your bracelet too—
    Thousands of patients and some with the flu.
Don't be late—sit and wait.
    Pharmacists, Social Workers, Psychiatrists—all doing great!
Cardiologists and surgeons (kindly and wise),
    Therapists, helping you to exercise.
"Slave drivers," "Bloodsuckers"—all with a goal—
    Body, mind and spirit once again whole.
Medical wonders, the latest equipment too—
    Top of the line is all that will do.
Syncardia Artificial Heart means you're tied to "Big Blue."

Aiming for a Freedom Driver—VAD techs, speech
therapists—"moo, boo, goo."
He's getting stronger,
so now our walks are longer.
Mennonite girls showing compassion, grace and love,
—Singing for patients, turning thoughts to God above.
Many heart transplants succeeded, organ donors always needed;
Gift of Life won't go unheeded, nor God's sovereignty
impeded.
Prayers and miracles abound and hope is found—
"The Mayo Story", but to God be the glory!
-Marilyn Hilkemann

"The message of the houses is simple for all of us: to offer love and
compassion to those who are going through some of the most difficult
medical treatments known. They leave their communities, their families
and their friends and come to cities where they know no one. These houses
become their support. We laugh and cry together, we offer a shoulder to
cry on and tremendous encouragement. We are a community of
healing. Ed and Jayne embraced this personally and made a mark on their
world. We all desire to do the same."
-Valerie Callahan, Executive Director of Gabriel's House

"The best thing I ever did was take care of Ed."
-Dr. Carl Anderson

Appendices

Our Gift of Life Transplant House - A home that helps and heals and so much more

By Dianna Dotson, 2014

Our Gift of Life journey began May 25, 2012, with Kevin's double lung transplant. Like all transplants our hope was to eventually make infrequent follow-up visits to Mayo Clinic, but for us that was not to be. It has been during these frequent visits I have asked myself, *What makes this house so special?* Is it the board, the staff, the volunteers, or the guests?

Or is it something within the very house itself? The board members change; we have seen new faces at the front desk and guests are checking in and out. So does our hope, our healing come from within these walls—these very walls that make up the house that we now call our "home away from home"?

My guess is a combination of all those things makes for a healing house.

Through the board's efforts the Gift of Life Transplant House is able to keep our room rates low. For this Kevin and I will be forever grateful, as we were not sure how we would be able to afford our frequent visits.

The staff and many volunteers provide us with much more than well-run houses, more than clean rooms that are ready for our return, more than a meal served after a long day, and more than the plentiful treats that await us in the kitchen. They give us their friendship, support, and encouragement. A warm smile greets us on our return and a gentle hug gives us a boost of strength just when we need it most.

Then there is *us*... the guests—both patients and caregivers. We are constantly revolving, checking in and checking out. Our stories are all different yet very much the same. Life has delivered us an unexpected, unplanned, and unwanted blow. Our journeys have brought us to the Mayo Clinic where some will need transplants, others will be caregivers but we will all need a place to call home.

In August 2013 Kevin underwent surgery in hopes of solving the problems he had been having with his lungs. After a long day at St. Marys I was at the Gift of Life doing dishes when I heard the crying. A caregiver had entered the kitchen and was sobbing....

"He doesn't even know who I am," she said.

My first thought was, *Please Lord be with this woman and her family and give them strength*. My second thought was, *I don't want to deal with this right now*, and I was glad another caregiver was holding her and offering comfort.

But after a few minutes I turned around and held out my arms and hugged her and listened. Because that's what we do here at the Gift of Life. That's our job—to be there to comfort and support each another.

At our Gift of Life the staff knows us and cares for us. After finding out in October that Kevin had R.A.S. and his new lungs were restricting, I left the hospital and came back to the house to get something. Tanya was there and she listened to my anger through my tears and offered just enough of a hug... But not too much of one because she knew for me, now was not the time.

The first person I called to share this news was not our family but our transplant family... Greg and Linda. They are our best friends forever, met here at the Gift of Life. Greg seemed to know what to say, what to ask, and not what to. It's hard to explain this bond we share but in some ways the people we meet here become closer to us than the family and friends we've known for years.

At our Gift of Life John and Bennie return for appointments at Mayo and find out John is much sicker than they thought and he is hospitalized. It is then that Ginger calls Greg and Linda because she had witnessed their friendship grow and saw how close they had become during their previous stay, and she knows Greg will want to say goodbye to John. Ginger also knows they will need one another and she is right—and Bennie is so grateful.

At our Gift of Life after Bob and Jan find out nothing else can be done—Bob's cancer is back and he doesn't have much time left—hospice is brought in and Bob is allowed to die within these walls. This is what he wants. The Gift of Life Transplant House after all has become "our home away from home"

Only at our Gift of Life do I pray for good news for Edward, only to find out it's not. I hold his mother as she tells me the news and we cry together knowing her son is going to die. Then fifteen minutes later I am with Edward, listening to him as he shares with me his plans to fight this anyhow, to try this new diet to maybe even seek treatment in Spain. I listen to Edward, I encourage him and I hold him tight... Then when I hear of his passing, I change my ringtone to one like his because I can't seem to forget him.

At our Gift of Life when I tell Steve that Kevin and I will be returning every other week for treatments and I jokingly ask if he has a spot for some of our stuff so we wouldn't have to haul it back and forth his response is, *Yes I will find a place to store it*, and he means it.

At our Gift of Life I am allowed to rearrange the Tupperware cupboard, help Cory move a desk, argue with Steve about the craft room and rake the front yard because they know that Dianna sometimes goes a little stir-crazy.

At our Gift of Life there are those of us that have had our transplants and now have complications. We are here often and now we get to encourage, cheer, listen, laugh, and hug those whose transplant journeys are just beginning. How very fortunate we are that our journeys can begin and sometimes end at the Gift of Life Transplant House, a home that offers...

Hope: when we have little
Comfort: on difficult days
Friendships: to brighten our spirits
And
Laughter: because after all laughter is the best medicine

Our journey takes us to a world that is completely foreign to us. A world where we are educated on medications we can barely pronounce. We learn about things like rejection, creatinine levels, graft vs. host, and we learn how much we dislike Prednisone.

After long days at Mayo we come home to our Gift of Life and it is here where we share, we support and encourage each other. We laugh, cry, and pray with one another. Lifelong friendships are made—when we leave this house we take with us new friends who understand the blessings, the joys, and also the fears and uncertainties that transplant brings to our lives. It is a bond that can't be broken and few understand.

Then there is the house itself...

I know how I feel each time I walk through those front doors. Sometimes I am alone because Kevin was admitted to St. Marys, but if I listen closely I imagine the voices of those who are no longer here and I smile. As I stand there I feel the comfort, the peace, the hope of the house almost as if the very walls themselves have greeted me and welcomed me home.

The founding of the Arizona Transplant House, as told by Tom Davie
August 2015

I met Ed through my wife, Mary Davie, when the first Gift of Life Transplant House was established in 1984. Mary was a member of the founding board of directors and was assigned the responsibility of securing volunteers to refurbish and organize the Center Street house. I was one of those volunteers who spent many hours cleaning, removing wallpaper, painting, hauling furniture etc. to get the house ready for guests. These volunteer efforts continued through the moves to the convent at St. John's Church and the Judd House. While many of us were doing the volunteer work of moving, renovating and organizing the various facilities, Ed was out raising the needed funds to pay off loans and secure funding for the added expenses of expanding the mission of Gift of Life Transplant House.

In 1997 Mary accepted a temporary position at the Mayo Clinic in Scottsdale, Arizona. At that time Mayo was building a new hospital in Phoenix, Arizona which was projected to open in 1998. When Mary arrived at Mayo in Arizona she was contacted by some of the medical personnel who were aware of the work she had done in helping start the Gift of Life Transplant House. Mayo Arizona was establishing a transplant program at the new hospital and wanted to have a facility in AZ that would provide housing for the transplant patients and their caregivers similar to the Gift of Life Transplant House in Rochester. Ultimately Mary accepted a position in the department of Human Resources at Mayo Clinic Arizona in 1998 and we made the decision that I would take early retirement from my administrative position with the Rochester, MN public schools and we would relocate to Arizona. Mary and I commuted back and forth from AZ to MN for a year and during that time Mary helped establish a volunteer board of directors for a Transplant House in AZ and began the task of finding a suitable facility.

Mary became aware of a large property in Scottsdale, AZ known as the Brusally Ranch that had been donated to Mayo in 1994 by a generous benefactor and Mayo was uncertain how they would use the property as it had been unoccupied for four years. This was a six-acre property with a large Spanish Colonial style house that had been part of a 160 acre Arabian horse ranch. Mary toured the property with a co-worker from Human Resources, Dana Cummings, and found that it would make a perfect Transplant House. The main house consisted of six bedrooms and a separate guesthouse each with a private bathroom, the house was built in the early 1950's.

Mary contacted Mayo AZ administration and inquired if it would be possible to use the property for a transplant house. After some intense negotiations with Mayo AZ administration, Facilities Department and the newly formed board of directors it was agreed that Mayo AZ would give the board a one year lease, for $ 1.00 per year, and if the project was successful after the first year the lease would be renewed. Mayo AZ also agreed to provide funds to do some plumbing upgrades, carpet, paint, grounds cleanup etc. It was then up to the board members and volunteers to prepare the house for occupancy. Furniture, kitchen items, linens paper products etc. had to be secured and the entire house cleaned from top to bottom.

I was again recruited as a volunteer to help with all the tasks needed to get the house ready for occupancy. The new transplant house became known as the Arizona Transplant House.

By this time I had been retired for about six months and found that I really did not like retirement too much and needed something more to do. I called Mary at work one day and asked what the board was thinking about who was going to manage the new transplant house. She said they did not have anyone in mind and there was no money available to hire someone. I said I would volunteer to manage the property since I had been around transplant houses for some time and believed I could help them get started. My offer was to volunteer for two/three months to get everything set up; accounting, registration procedures etc. Mary took my offer to the board and they accepted it and the house was opened for patients/caregivers on July 1, 1999. I consulted with Sr. Margeen Hoffman at Rochester Gift of Life many times and established operational procedures/guidelines consistent with them and modeled the operation based on the success of Gift of Life.

It soon became apparent that the Arizona Transplant House was an integral part of the success of the transplant program at Mayo Clinic Arizona. The seven rooms of the House were nearly always filled to capacity. My two/three month volunteer offer ultimately turned into a full-time paid position and I was named

Executive Director in 2001. The one-year lease with Mayo was extended for five years and five more after that. The success of the project was evident.

Mary was elected President of the Arizona Transplant House Board of Directors in 2003. In 2007 the board began discussing the need to expand the Arizona Transplant House as the need for housing of transplant patients was growing and projected to continue. There were discussions of expanding on the present six acre site since the property was located exactly between the Mayo Clinic in Scottsdale and the Mayo Hospital in Phoenix. Mayo AZ Administration decided they wanted to have their hospitality house programs close to the Mayo Hospital in Phoenix, AZ and made the decision to sell the Brusally Ranch property. This sale was completed by Mayo in 2007 and the proceeds were used to build a new facility on the hospital campus.

A unique relationship was established with Mayo AZ leadership and the Mayo AZ Department of Development. Mayo agreed to raise the funds from generous benefactors to build the houses plus the administration/community center and the Arizona Transplant House Board was responsible to secure funds and donations of furniture to operate the houses. The property and the houses were leased to AZTH for the sum of $1.00 per year. We enjoyed tremendous support and encouragement from Mayo physicians, administrators, development officers, Clinic and hospital allied staff as well as the patients and caregivers who stayed at the facility.

This new facility consisted of three individual houses, each with six bedrooms/baths, common living, dining, kitchen patio etc. In addition to the houses there was a large administration/community center that was separate from the houses. The mission was expanded to include cancer patients in addition to the transplant patients. The first phase of the new facility, administration/community center and three houses, was completed in June, 2009 with a total of 18 bedrooms. In 2011 one more six bedroom house was completed and in 2013 a two-story house with 12 bedrooms was completed making a total of 36 rooms. The new facility is known as the Village at Mayo Clinic-Arizona Transplant House

From the time the first AZ transplant house was opened Mary and I maintained our relationship with Ed and Jayne Pompeian and received encouragement and support from them. They visited the Arizona facilities several times and were pleased to see that the model of the Rochester Gift of Life Transplant House was being replicated. Ed and I also served together on the board of directors for the National Association of Hospital Hospitality Houses, now changed to Hospital Hospitality Network.

Soon after the Arizona Transplant House was established in 1999 discussions began with a small group of people who were operating a hospitality house in Jacksonville, Florida. Mayo Administrative leadership in Florida also wanted to have a transplant house on the Mayo Florida campus to serve their transplant patients. Staff members visited the Rochester Gift of Life and the Arizona Transplant House to see how they were operated. In 2011 the 30 room Gabriel House of Care was established on the Mayo Florida Campus. What Ed and the founding board of directors of Gift of Life started in 1984 is now replicated on Mayo campuses in Arizona and Florida. The Rochester Gift of Life Transplant House became the gold standard for hospital hospitality houses around the United States.

Mary continued to serve as President of the Board of AZTH until 2013. She and I worked closely with the board to fulfill the mission of providing a comfortable, cost effective, home-like environment for transplant patients and their caregivers from the Southwest United States and beyond.

From 1999 to 2007 I was the only paid staff person with the exception of a part time housekeeper. We also had a dedicated group of volunteers who assisted with house operations and grounds keeping. In 2007 Dana Cummings, (mentioned earlier when she arranged for Mary to tour the Brusally Ranch House), was hired as operations manager. When we moved to the new facility on the hospital campus we had a staff of 7 full and part time employees. The program had grown very rapidly those first 10 years.

My two/three month volunteer position expanded into 15 years of the most rewarding work I have ever done. Sr. Margeen told me very early on that I would find the work I was doing a ministry and she could not have been more accurate. I retired from the Village at Mayo Clinic-Arizona Transplant House in April 2014.

Please consider becoming an organ donor

When I had my first transplant the process was still very much in the experimental phase. I often think of those talented and dedicated researchers and the brave patients who took those first risky steps in what's become a long and fruitful history of transplant research. There were thousands of people who literally risked their lives in the hopes that someone would benefit—even if they themselves did not.

Today, the Mayo Clinic has one of the most successful transplant programs in the world. Thousands of procedures are performed every year in Rochester, Jacksonville, and Scottsdale. Participation in the transplant program has saved countless lives. By simply becoming an organ donor you can make your own gift of life, and help so many people and their families. Please visit the Gift of Life Transplant House and the Mayo Clinic online to learn more:

http://gift-of-life.org/

http://www.mayoclinic.org/